safari
South
America

TAPLINGER PUBLISHING COMPANY
NEW YORK

safari South America

CHRISTINA WOOD

ILLUSTRATED BY
NANCY LOU GAHAN

First published in the United States in 1973 by
TAPLINGER PUBLISHING CO., INC.
New York, New York

Originally published in Great Britain in 1972
as *The Magic Sakis*

Library of Congress Catalog Card Number: 73–1764

ISBN 0–8008–6945–1

2/27/74

Contents

Illustrations

Author's Note

When considering the dedication of this book—an act of ambiguous generosity which few new authors can resist—an embarrassing multitude of people sprang to mind; so many who helped and encouraged me in so many ways.

But then I remembered a group of firemen who, with nonchalant courage and cheerfulness, rescued several of us trapped at the top of a burning hotel on the night of December 26th 1963. A fireman's lot is not only dirty, dangerous and largely thankless, but also frustrating to anyone with even a modicum of curiosity; almost never does he learn what happens to the lives he saves.

This time, with my thanks, the lads of Maida Vale Fire Station can hear the end of the story. Their timely assistance not only made this book physically possible, but it also inadvertently set me upon the jungle trail.

My special thanks also to Guyana's Tourist Officer, M. Insan Ali, friend, adviser, and problem-solver *par excellence*, for his endurance and humour under a continual bombardment of requests.

Christina Wood

1

The Trail to the Jungle

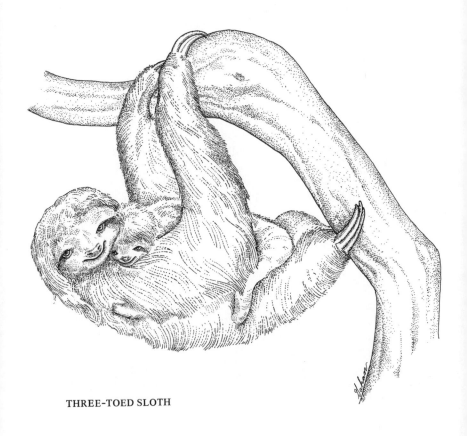

THREE-TOED SLOTH

There was nothing to warn me that my life was about to alter course as I caught a train from Twickenham to Waterloo on a warm sunny morning in May 1965. We were having an early heat-wave, and the unexpected warmth and cheerful brilliance of the sunshine seemed to add sparkle to everyone's eyes and an extra spring to their step. I had no inkling that within a short time I would be sweltering in the heat of a jungle swamp.

Fifteen months before this I had been trapped in an hotel fire. I had spent twenty-four hours in hospital after I was rescued, and should probably have done better to remain in hospital for a while, for within a day of discharging myself I suffered delayed shock and for several months I had to fight an unadmitted nervous breakdown. I had lost everything in the fire. The spurt of joy I had felt in finding my life intact after the fire had soon dispersed when faced with the sheer difficulty of living from day to day, hungry, frightened, insecure and ill. But now the memory of that time that had lain constantly and painfully at the back of my mind like a dark cloud began at last to lift. I was twenty-nine years old and beginning to earn, by my modest standards, quite a lot of money from freelance journalism. Now the sun was shining and I had money in the bank; it was suddenly good to be alive.

After I left home at seventeen I had had seven years on a farm, totally absorbed in animals and the countryside. Then I had moved to London, and in my flat had gradually acquired a toy poodle, Pinto, a baby marmoset and an increasing number of tropical animals: flying squirrels, foreign finches, salamanders, tree-frogs, toads, chameleons, terrapins, lizards and a baby alligator. At last I had found something that utterly absorbed me. My flat in St John's Wood rang with the noise of them; in particular the tropical-sounding pulsing cry of the frogs at night was the cause of much puzzlement to passers-by.

In the beginning I made the mistake of thinking that my experience in looking after domestic and farm animals could be applied to exotic animals. But strangely enough this principle doesn't work.

I had to 'get the feel' of caring for tropical animals, and it was a long time developing. It wasn't, in fact, until I started to deal with a great many tropical animals some years later that I suddenly found that I had acquired this 'feel', best described as thinking myself into the animal's shoes with half my mind, while remaining a watchful observer with the other half. This has enabled me to keep very delicate animals alive, healthy and happy, and this in turn has built up my confidence, so that I am continually aiming higher in my zoological ambitions. But in those early days at St John's Wood, I was only a fumbling amateur, trying to do my best but continually making mistakes.

Most of my writing concerned animals, and my journey that day in May was to attend the Annual General Meeting of the International Society for the Protection of Animals. I was interested in a wildlife-rescue, Operation Gwamba, that they had started in Surinam, South America, where a bush-Negro team, led by a wild American, John Walsh, were rescuing several thousand wild animals trapped by the rising waters of a hydro-electric dam in a jungle valley. ISPA'S Chief Administrator for the Western Hemisphere, J. Robert Smith, would be at the meeting on one of his infrequent visits to England from Boston, Massachusetts, and as he had visited Operation Gwamba's jungle camp I hoped that a talk with him would provide me with material for an article for the *Sunday Express*.

When the official meeting was over I managed to corner Bob Smith, a burly silver-haired American with a quiet sense of humour. He resigned himself willingly enough to answer my endless questions, and we began to sort through a large pile of photographs of the rescue operation. Bob invited me to continue our discussion at a private cocktail party being given by ISPA's President the following evening at the Savoy Hotel, which delegates of the Society from all over the world would be attending. And it was in the splendid but highly unlikely surroundings of the Savoy that I suddenly saw a clearly-blazed trail leading straight to the jungle I'd hankered after for years.

The next evening was warm and sultry, and the immaculate white summer suits of the many Americans present, sandwiched between the deep-piled carpets and the crystal chandeliers, made me feel I was watching a Hollywood production rather than actually taking part in the proceedings. Beyond

11

the big windows London's lights reflected mistily on the Thames, and an illuminated river-steamer glided by in the falling dusk.

In between introducing me to countless people, Bob continued telling me about Surinam.

'It's a great country, if you like that sort of thing,' he said. 'I prefer some comfort myself, but John Walsh is crazy about living right out in the jungle. I couldn't see much fun sleeping in a hammock in an open-sided hut, with swarms of insects, poisonous snakes, vampire bats, lousy food and never anything cold to drink even in that heat. The water's typhoid-infected, so you get a choice of two drinks, medicated coffee or medicated luke-warm water.'

His face was incredulous as he remembered the indignities and discomforts he had suffered.

'You know what we had to eat twice a day? Rice and pigs' tails! John's still out there living on that diet, Heaven help him. It's a beautiful country, though. Wild orchids everywhere, and huge purple butterflies. The jungle is so thick you have to cut a way through with a machete. And the rapids roaring down through the rocks on the river are really something.'

'It sounds wonderful,' I answered, my mind far away imagining it all. 'The type of place I've always wanted to go to.'

Bob looked startled for a moment, and then laughed indulgently. 'That's no place for a woman,' he said.

'Why?' I asked, more curious than offended.

'Well . . .' he floundered for a moment. 'It just isn't. It's hot and dirty and disease-ridden and dangerous. Not a woman's kind of country. Not,' he amended with misplaced gallantry, 'a woman like you, at any rate.'

I suppressed the temptation to tell him that, elegant black cocktail dress this evening notwithstanding, I had gone charring for a living every morning for the past fifteen months since becoming destitute after the fire. My writing was only part of my income, performed in the evenings. Only a couple of hours before arriving at the Savoy I had been scrubbing someone's kitchen floor. I was no lady, as it were; I was a charlady. Instead, I misguidedly mentioned what I considered a more respectable occupation.

'You know, I spent seven years working a farm, milking forty head of cattle, driving tractors, and so on. Muck-spreading in the fields and castrating piglets may not be a ladylike occupation, but I got along with them all right.'

Bob choked over his drink and there was a startled pool of silence from the people standing nearest us.

'So I don't see why,' I persisted, 'the jungle should be thought no place for a woman.'

At that moment we were joined by Trevor Scott, a dark handsome young man who was Chief Administrator for the Eastern Hemisphere. He had spent some years with the Royal Society for the Prevention of Cruelty to Animals in West Africa, and Bob appealed to him rather helplessly for support in his argument.

'You tell her, Trevor. The jungle's okay for a man, but it's much too tough for a girl.'

'Oh, I'm sure you wouldn't like it,' Trevor said with polite earnestness. 'The jungle may seem glamorous and exciting in a book or film, but the reality is thousands of biting insects, every kind of disease you can think of, and a good deal of danger.'

'You didn't like the jungle, then?' I asked.

'Oh, I loved it!' he said enthusiastically, and then stopped abruptly as he realised he was contradicting his own words. He grinned as he explained unnecessarily, 'But then, I'm not a girl.'

During the next hour my contribution to the conversation was absent-minded. I had suddenly realised that here was my long-awaited opportunity to see the jungle. But the whole idea seemed so enormous and outlandish, particularly in these high society surroundings, that frankly it frightened me a little. But scared or not, I couldn't turn away from a chance like this.

'Bob,' I said as soon as there was a quiet moment, 'would you let me stay in Operation Gwamba's camp for a few weeks?'

'You don't want to do that!' he said, shocked.

'Oh, yes, I do,' I replied firmly, although a little flutter of

13

apprehension in the region of my solar plexus tried to deny it.

He looked at me thoughtfully, wondering how serious I was.

'You need press publicity to get public funds, don't you?' I prompted.

'It all helps,' he admitted reluctantly.

'I'd pay my own expenses, of course, but I think I'd get most of my outlay back from writing articles about the wild-life-rescue. I really would like to go out there, if there's room for me to stay in the camp,' I added persuasively.

'There's plenty of room,' Bob said slowly, 'along with the vampire bats, scorpions, snakes and all the rest.'

Deciding that I should have forgotten all about it by the next morning, he rashly promised, 'I dare say I could fix it up with John Walsh for you to stay there, if you really want to.'

The night was very beautiful and still as I took a taxi back to Twickenham, having missed the last train. We mounted an unusually deserted Richmond Hill in bright moonlight. It was a splendid setting for the important decision I had to make. I felt both exhilaration and trepidation; I just couldn't make up my mind. For years I'd been dreaming of jungles, a senseless-seeming dream, perhaps, but a very definite one. But now that the chance to go had fallen into my lap all kinds of arguments against it presented themselves.

If I went to Surinam it would mean gambling all the money that, to me miraculously, I had managed to earn by writing far into every night. Without that money in the bank I should feel vulnerable. But I had to do it, or miss what was probably my one chance in a lifetime to do exactly what I wanted. I *had* to go.

When I reached home I took an atlas to bed with me, and found Surinam sandwiched between French and British Guiana, north of Brazil. I spent the remainder of the night trying to pluck up enough courage. Two days later I sent a cable to Bob Smith, who had gone back to Boston. It read:

REQUEST PERMISSION STAY SEVERAL WEEKS ISPA CAMP SURINAM STOP MAGAZINE INTERESTED

14

After a few days, full of suspense now that I had finally made up my mind, I received a cautious cable from Bob:

VISIT CAN POSSIBLY BE ARRANGED STOP LETTER FOLLOWS

His letter reiterated every warning about the jungle he'd already given me, plus a few more. I replied that I was willing to accept existing conditions. Everything was arranged. I was going to the Surinam jungle for six weeks.

I had seven weeks to get ready and in my ignorance I thought this time would be more than ample. As I should be staying in Operation Gwamba's island camp, I didn't have the worry or expense of purchasing any basic equipment. But there were countless other preparations I had to make.

I visited the offices of several magazines and newspapers to give them a brief outline of the wildlife-rescue, and roused a fair amount of interest in my forthcoming articles. BBC radio, a new market for me, showed unexpected enthusiasm for the subject, and it was arranged that I should make a half-hour programme for the Home Service on my return from Surinam, and perhaps a short talk for Woman's Hour.

On-the-spot tape-recordings would be an important part of the programme. An obliging technician at the BBC gave me a crash course in the art of making outside sound recordings. As I'd never used a tape-recorder in my life, his advice was more than valuable.

There were dozens of other time-consuming tasks: obtaining a passport, visas, health certificate, endless and painful inoculations for smallpox, typhoid, typhus, tetanus and yellow fever, air flights to book, travellers' cheques to collect, and light-weight clothes for town and jungle to buy.

Suddenly my trip was on, although I really only half believed it; I felt sure something would happen to stop my going. I had never flown in an aeroplane before, and in the week before my departure there were three air crashes. The weather on the day of my departure was depressing. Although it was early July the wind drove the rain obliquely across the tarmac at London Airport, and grey clouds sat low in the sky. My Boeing 707 roared down the runway, then swooped up almost vertically into the low clouds. I sat wordlessly hold-

15

ing my stomach; I had somehow imagined the ascent would be slow and gentle.

I was travelling first to Boston, where I would spend a day and a half fixing up the last details of publicity with Bob Smith at ISPA's head office. It had been 44° fahrenheit in London; it was 83° when I arrived in Boston and found Bob waiting to whisk me off to lunch. Due to the hour-change I had already had two breakfasts and one lunch, but as it was still only 1 p.m. local time Bob logically believed I must be ready for a meal and insisted that I quell my hunger with my first-ever enormous American steak, followed by a great dish of ice-cream.

Dazed by the effects of travelling, too much food and drink and the fiercely hot sunshine, I was then caught up in a wider circle of overwhelming American hospitality. A friendly motorcade eventually delivered me back to my hotel just after midnight.

Next day I was taken over every department of the Boston SPCA Animal Hospital, perhaps the finest in the world. The social evening ahead included a barbecue with more huge and succulent steaks. I was delivered back to the hotel at 2 a.m., and managed to snatch two hours' sleep before leaving for the airport to catch the dawn flight for South America. I love the Americans, but as I found both then and since, I have to be a hundred per cent fit before I can survive their friendship.

Travelling south on the 'island-hop' the temperature increased gradually and the humidity rapidly. By the time we reached Port-of-Spain in Trinidad I was exhausted. I sat in the airport lounge while the ground staff refuelled, watching the jungle hills vanishing as darkness descended. The moisture-laden air seemed to stifle me, and I had to force my eyes to stay open until the Jet Clipper was ready to complete the last two short legs of our journey to Surinam. A middle-aged American took a seat beside me in the lounge and said sympathetically, 'Not used to the heat?'

Apparently I looked as hot and tired as I felt. His own tanned skin was dry and he looked unflustered by the oppressive atmosphere. He told me he lived in Surinam and looked momentarily startled when I said that was my own destination. For a moment curiosity struggled with good manners,

16

but curiosity won and he asked me the reason for my visit.

'You see, we don't often get lone women arriving in a place like Surinam,' he explained.

I told him I was writing some articles and making a radio programme about Operation Gwamba.

'I'm going out to the island camp for a few weeks,' I continued, but he interrupted with great concern.

'*What?* Do you have any idea what it's like out there?'

'I think so. I know it's tough, if that's what you mean.'

'Well, as long as you know what you're doing,' he said doubtfully. 'I'm surprised John Walsh agreed to it, though. It's no place for a woman out there.'

'You know John Walsh, then?' I asked.

'Oh, sure,' Mr Sweig said. He grinned suddenly. 'I guess everyone in Surinam knows John Walsh. He's as crazy as they come.'

We reached Paramaribo Airport nearly two hours later. Dazed with tiredness I was glad to let Mr Sweig guide me through immigration and customs. Then he kindly shared his taxi with me on the twenty-mile journey to the capital. When I reached the Torarica Hotel, where I had booked a room, I told the desk clerk not to call me in the morning. Bob had said it would probably be four or five days before John Walsh could come into town to collect me, and I was glad now of the opportunity to rest and get acclimatised before the real work started.

Nine o'clock next morning I was woken by the shrill summons of the telephone beside my bed. Still half-asleep I picked up the receiver and mumbled into it. A deep, growly voice with a Boston accent spoke abruptly.

'John Walsh here. I'm downstairs. Look, I just got into town to pick up supplies and found a cable from Bob Smith saying you were coming last night.'

I sat up, shaking myself awake. I felt at a distinct disadvantage, still lounging in bed while John Walsh had already made the four-hour journey into town from the camp.

'I don't know why you want to come out to my camp,' John Walsh was complaining. 'I can't have women wandering about out there, it's too dangerous. Anyway, you'd best come down now and we'll talk about it.'

17

Five minutes later I was walking into the hotel's coffee bar where John said he would be waiting. Most of the people in there were American businessmen or tourists, some in white suits and others in immaculate shorts and vivid shirts. Only one man could possibly be John Walsh, a black-bearded fellow with sharply intelligent eyes, dressed in faded jeans and a patched check shirt and leaning his six-foot-four frame on the counter casually while he chatted to the pretty waitress. There was no hint of friendliness in his expression as we shook hands. He was more than a foot taller than I, and I felt like a small errant child appearing before the headmaster.

'You want coffee?' he offered abruptly.

I hesitated. 'I'd rather have tea.'

He grunted in disgust and ordered tea for me. When it came I told him I wanted to come out to the island to make recordings for the programme, photographs for the articles and to obtain material for both by seeing details of how the animals were being rescued from the hundreds of submerging islands. John's stiff hostility began to fade, although he was obviously still unhappy about taking a girl out to his camp.

'How long do you want to come for?' he asked at last.

'It depends how soon I get the material I want. About six weeks, I'd say.'

'Six weeks?' He looked at me with shocked incredulity. 'I can't have a girl on my island for six weeks! You wouldn't last out there for more than a few days. It's no joy-ride, you know.'

I already had a fairly accurate idea of the conditions on the islands, but John gave me some further details. Normal living jungle is, on the whole, a reasonably safe place if one uses a little commonsense and care. It doesn't swarm with venomous snakes and other dangers; although these things exist, it is quite possible to go several weeks at a time without even getting a glimpse of them.

But John was working in a dead and dying jungle, and conditions were vastly different from normal. As the flood-water for the dam slowly rose in the eight-hundred-square-mile forested valley, the wild animals took to the high ground. Some found themselves in safety on the fringe of the mainland, with hundreds of miles of green jungle lying before them. But thousands of other animals were not so lucky. The high ground they chose in the valley became surrounded with water, isolating several hundred small newly-formed islands from the safe mainland.

As the months passed the water rose a few inches each day, and the islands shrank even smaller, the lowest ones soon disappearing silently beneath the lake. The wildlife of the forest was concentrated in the ever-decreasing areas of dry ground—not only mammals but also snakes and scorpions and other dangerous insects. These were the places that John and his team of bush-Negroes hunted each day, and the camp was one of the smaller islands twenty-five miles from the mainland. Unlike the living jungle, these islands literally crawled with venomous snakes.

The trapped animals had no chance of trying to swim to the mainland, for there were packs of piranha roaming in the lake. Except for the few that took to the water and quickly perished, the animals stayed and eventually began to starve as they stripped the dying trees of foliage. Flocks of vampire bats attacked the weakened animals each night, weakening them still further through loss of blood. Each island was surrounded by thick half-submerged forest, and the boats had to be forced through what had once been the forest canopy, now dead and rotting and full of insects that fell into the boat as the branches were disturbed. The rescue work was hard and dirty and dangerous. An average of three boats a week capsized through colliding with submerged logs, or from rotten trees falling on top of them.

The lake was stagnant from the mass of waterlogged vegetation, virtually a swamp, and under these conditions disease took a hold. The lake water was typhoid-infected, and although drinking water was imported from the mainland, the lake still had to be used for washing purposes.

The animals had been thrown into a state of fear by finding themselves trapped. Some species, like jaguar and ocelot, were in no danger of starving but nevertheless had to be rescued before the water rose high enough to drown them. Other species, tree porcupine, agouti, armadillo, deer, paca, sloth, monkey, tamandua anteater, and many others, all normally peaceful animals, were terrified and fought tooth and nail when captured.

'It's really tough out there,' John concluded, 'and I don't have time to be nursemaid to a girl.'

I had a feeling that, in his shoes, I'd be feeling the same reluctance about getting landed with someone who'd never been in the jungle before. But his remark about being a nursemaid stung me. I swallowed my irritation and said reasonably, 'I know you've got a difficult and important job to do, and I'll make sure I don't get in your way. I'll just follow along behind and take recordings and watch what you do.'

He scratched his ear worriedly. 'Okay, then. I'll come back for you in an hour. Don't bring too much stuff with you. The boat's already overloaded and I don't want to sink it.'

With a brief gesture of farewell he went with long strides to the door. He stopped and turned as a sudden thought struck him.

'I suppose you can swim?'

'Yes.'

'Just as well,' he said ominously.

2
Camp Life

That was when the real magic began, on the long, tough journey into the interior. John drove his huge long-wheelbase Land-rover truck at high speed along the new red-raw highway that had been carved out of the rugged land leading south, then took a short cut on a rutted track leading across the savannah to the head of the Afobaka Dam. The sparse scrubland gradually gave way to the true tropical forest, where giant trees with unfamiliar leaves trailed long wigs of hanging moss and lianas.

The cooling system for the Land-rover's engine began to play up, and as the gauge needle rose John brought the truck to a halt in the shade of some trees near a small creek. He stripped off his shirt and disappeared beneath the truck, while I sat down by the creek and tried to quell the steadily rising excitement I was feeling with each new mile that was placing us farther from the town and nearer the jungle.

I didn't offer to help John, although after several years of driving tractors on a hill farm I had a fair talent for fixing malingering engines. But John was a giant of a man and I knew that nothing but a guffaw of derision would greet an offer of help from someone of my puny stature.

The sun beat down on my head like a furnace, but it was far more bearable than the intense humidity of Trinidad the night before. Within fifteen minutes John had finished the repairs. He squirmed out from under the truck and carefully shook his shirt before he started putting it on.

When he saw me watching him, he said, 'One of the first things you've got to learn to do out here is shake your clothes and tip up your shoes before you put them on.'

'Scorpions?' I asked.

'And tarantulas and a few dozen other poisonous insects, plus the odd snake,' he said drily.

As he buttoned up his shirt he told me of something that had happened to him during his first week in the jungle fifteen months before. At that time he had had to stop on the savannah trail to make a similar quick repair to the truck, and as he was alone he had taken off his jeans as well as his shirt so that they didn't get oil on them, and had thrown them in a heap on the ground.

With nobody to teach him the simple precautions necessary

for living in the tropical interior, he hadn't thought to shake his clothes when he came to put them on half an hour later. He pulled on his jeans and was just fastening them when he realised that something large, fat and furry was crawling on his thigh inside the denim material. His action was instinctive but ill-advised. He slapped his hand down hard on the lump, clenching his teeth as he felt the monstrous insect simultaneously bite him as it died from the blow.

He ripped his trousers off and found a red tarantula spider as big as my hand. His thigh was already inflamed and swollen from the poison, and for two days John felt ill and acutely uncomfortable with the pain. The poison of the black tarantula is fairly mild, but the red tarantula is capable of killing a child or anyone who is already in poor health. The bite of this big red one left John with quite a bad scar on his thigh where much of the skin died off from the effects of the poison.

'So one thing I never forget is shaking out my clothes,' he concluded as we climbed back into the cab.

I pulled a face. 'Spiders are one thing I don't much like,' I confessed. 'Snakes I don't mind, nor scorpions, vampire bats and all the rest. Just so long as I don't meet up with too many spiders, particularly furry tarantulas.'

'Oh, you will,' John assured me cheerfully. 'In fact I've got a pet black tarantula in my hut—I'll introduce you to him when we reach camp!'

When we reached Afobaka, John brought the truck to a stop thirty feet back from the edge of the lake.

'Afobaka means half-way back,' he said conversationally.

I looked around us. To the north was the isolated scrubland through which we had just passed; to the south, east and west was the drowned forest valley, and beyond it in the distance were the hills where the thick green jungle began.

'Half-way back from where?' I asked, puzzled.

'Nobody knows,' he grinned, 'and that about sums up this crazy country.'

The dam was impressive: great saddle-dykes and a giant 218-foot high concrete spillway; but the acres of bull-dozed land around us were barren of vegetation and the deep red of the earth looked raw and bleeding. Although it was a

23

tribute to man's feats of engineering, the scene somehow gave a painful impression of brute-force.

I had expected the lake, eight-hundred miles of flooded jungle, to present a view of utter devastation. But instead it had a curious beauty. The water at that time was about 180 feet deep and still rising. All the smaller trees of the forest had completely submerged in this part of the lake, but the crowns of the giant trees were still above the surface.

The brazenness had gone from the late afternoon sun, leaving the sky a pale washed blue. The gaunt skeletons of the trees still unsubmerged were every shade of soft silver and grey, sometimes tinged with a pale, ghostly green. The water beneath, the same gentle blue as the sky, was so still that every last detail of the leafless branches was reflected on its glassy surface. Here and there the heart of a giant palm still showed a flash of sharp green, a reminder of the luxuriant and colourful forest that now lay beneath the lake

I looked out across the drowning valley, and instead of seeing devastation I saw something as beautiful in its lifeless way as a winter snow scene, something that Surinam would never know. The branches, like arms held high, formed a delicate tracery for a panorama of muted pastel colours. It was sad to see the massive forest succumbing to the slow flood. Yet the strongest impression was of peace, for it died with a strange dignity and fragile beauty. I felt much farther from civilisation than the one hundred miles we had just travelled.

We travelled twenty-five miles across the lake in a motorised dugout canoe loaded with sacks of rice, vegetables and fruit that John had bought in Paramaribo. Several great drums of fuel made the boat lie even lower in the water, and we arranged ourselves gingerly amongst the supplies, careful not to rock the over-loaded boat.

The afternoon sun sank lower towards the far hills and sent an orange glow across the water as we glided steadily into the heart of the wasteland. The sky turned a vivid flame red behind the smoky black thunder clouds that were beginning to pile up, and I experienced one of those brief but unnerving moments of 'I've been here before.'

The fantasy fire of the sunset had faded as we approached the camp island. John cut the throttle and we drifted slowly through the shadowy dusk, wisps of white mist rising from the water around us. As the silhouette of the island loomed up in front of us I became aware of the acrid smell of wood-smoke, and saw thin white columns from a dozen cooking fires rising waveringly through the trees. Mixed with the wood smoke was the over-ripe and pungent smell of the jungle itself. The evening air was soft and moist on my smarting face, and the lake water slapped softly against the side of the boat as we slid silently to a mooring on the bank.

In the half-dark I could just see the outlines of twenty or thirty huts, simple structures of lashed poles topped with steeply-pitched roofs of palm leaves. But as I stepped out on to the bank it was neither the sight, nor the smell of the place that filled me with something approaching complete happiness. It was the sound of the jungle. Frogs, toads, crickets and dozens of other unknown insects, some with high-pitched voices and some that were low-pitched, all combined into an unsynchronised chorus that throbbed and clamoured incessantly. And, behind the pulse of the night creatures, the sound of drums beating. As I stood there I felt that I wouldn't complain if I got killed tomorrow; the most important thing was that I had reached the jungle.

My first few days living rough were not easy. Some things I was able to take in my stride; the danger, the lack of privacy from the forty men who lived on the island, sleeping in a hammock for the first time and the long working hours out in the boats, from six in the morning until four in the afternoon with seldom any break. Other things, such as the food and the heat, took more getting used to. The sun quickly blistered my face and the heat of the afternoons induced a feeling of heavy-eyed weariness, but within a few days my body acclimatised until at last I was even enjoying the hot sunny days. The food, an unappetising mess of rice and pigs' tails cooked by a young bush-Negro boy called Atimo, I found to be almost unedible, although I am not a fussy feeder. It always astonished me to see John consume a heaped plateful of it and then hand his plate to Atimo for a second helping. I had brought some secret stores with me, after Bob Smith's warning about the food, and to Atimo's fury I went about improving the taste of the rice and pigs' tails by adding liberal handfuls of Knorr packet soups, Paxo stuffing and chicken-stock cubes to the cooking pot.

But even so, I just could not face a plateful of it at five-thirty every morning, as well as in the evening. So I missed breakfast, we never got any lunch because we were out working on the lake, and my one meal of the day was not sufficient to stop me losing weight rapidly. As I weighed only seven and a half stone on arrival, I had little enough to lose. Then, to my joy, five days later I found a forgotten sack of porridge oats in the store shed. Although I had failed dismally in trying to teach Atimo how to make a good pot of tea (mainly because, in his eagerness to please, he would pour the heating water on to the tea leaves as soon as he saw me approach, not wanting to keep me waiting until the water boiled), we had better luck with the porridge, and he managed to produce a thick creamy plateful of it for me each morning.

So the food and the heat soon became unimportant details. But there were two other aspects of living in the jungle which I found much more difficult to overcome.

The first of these was the almost total lack of washing facilities. I'd spent a few years getting dirty for a living, dung-hauling, hay-making, and milking a herd of forty mud-plastered cows, but the difference then had been that at the end of each day there were unlimited gallons of fresh, clean water to wash the grime from me.

It was dirty work visiting the islands each day, as the boats had to be dragged through acres of dead tree tops in order to approach the dry land of each small island. Dust, insects and twigs descended in showers on to us, and our legs became caked with red mud when we clambered out of the boats and waded the last few yards. And all of us sweated, constantly and profusely. All this would have been bearable if there had been some way of getting really clean again at the end of each day.

But instead there was only the lake water: dark-brown, stagnant, smelly, full of filth and disease. We couldn't even bathe in the lake, which illogically would at least have given us the illusion of cleanliness, for the packs of piranha had been attracted to the island by the disposal of waste food and washing dishes in the shallows, and they constantly roamed a few yards off-shore.

So we washed out of buckets. Each evening I stared unwillingly into the murky depths of my bucketful of water, seeing the mass of tiny, wriggling insects, and smelling the stench of rotting vegetation. It hardly seemed worthwhile to wash, for the water was as dirty as I; but then the dust caking my lips, the grit grating against my damp, sticky skin and the furtive movements of tiny insects that had fallen down my neck all persuaded me otherwise.

The lack of washing facilities made me really miserable for nine or ten days, as it did with every new arrival on the island, mainly, I think, because of a very real mental conflict produced by having to abandon something we'd spent a lifetime believing to be a basic virtue—cleanliness. But the misery suddenly disappeared of its own accord, and the matter ceased to be of real importance. At least, I felt, we could all be dirty together.

But my second-stumbling block I hated to the bitter end, and I can only thank God that it was one I never subsequently met in normal living jungle. What was this jungle horror that kept me sleepless at night and wore down my resistance so relentlessly that I came almost to the point of giving up and returning to civilisation? Of all innocuous things, *fleas*—hundreds of them.

In his book about Operation Gwamba*, John later wrote:
'Of the insect pests, perhaps fleas took top honours, with ticks bucking for second place.... Nothing is so accursed, so maddening as the plague of fleas that descended upon us with the rainy season. They'd get down inside our underwear and their bites would be like tiny, red-hot pins. I'd lie in my hammock at night, waiting for the next one to hit, and when it did, in a frenzy I'd slap myself silly. Then I'd lie, tensed and expectant, waiting for the next one.'

In one way, unlike John, I was lucky, for there is something about my blood which ensures that ticks never bite me. Even the cow-ticks on the farm had never bothered me. Often I

---

* *Time is Short and the Water Rises* by John Walsh with Robert Gannon (Nelson, 1967).

would oblige John by picking a dozen or more swollen ticks off his back and shoulders.

The fleas on the island were no joke. They came off the wild animals, which were frequently caged in camp overnight before release on the mainland, and on to the pack of hunting dogs that were forever milling round our feet. And if the ticks had disdained me, the fleas considered me top quality grade one, and with one accord abandoned the dogs and adopted me.

Within three days they'd taken more bites off me than they took off John in all his months there. My back and shoulders, for some reason their favourite feasting patch, became one huge, swollen and festering sore. The irritation of it, especially at night, almost drove me insane. The fleas were by far the worst thing I have ever had to endure since in the jungle.

I fought back at them slowly and grimly. I'd always been a dog-lover, but nobody would have thought so now if they'd heard the way I snarled at any flea-ridden dog that came fawning round me as I sat in the kitchen hut in the evenings. Tying my trouser-legs tightly around my ankles cut off the favourite trail of the fleas. Most important of all was a thorough de-fleaing session before I crawled inside the mosquito-net into my hammock, for inadvertently locking a couple of fleas inside with me had been the cause of the terrible foot-square sore on my back. So each night I stripped off my dirty clothes, washed in the stagnant water, put on freshly-washed clothes ready for the next day's work, brushed out my long hair and quickly dived—flealess, I hoped—through the small entrance to the mosquito-net into my hammock, and with the drawstring closed the hole firmly after me. In this way I stopped the fleas massacring me, but it remained a running battle throughout my six weeks on the island, and I developed an almost neurotic loathing of fleas that has never left me.

'Chris learned to fit into camp life in only a few days,' John wrote in his book, 'and soon we got used to having to wear clothes all the time, watch our language, and drink English tea. After my initial sourness at having to put up with a woman around camp, I began to find it even pleasant for a change.'

It was a pretty good summing-up of our relationship in the first few days, with John alternately his normal cheerful self and having moods as sour as an unripe lemon, when he would mutter with quiet anguish in the depths of his black beard, 'I never thought I'd get landed with a girl out *here*!'

The question of where to accommodate me for the first few nights caused John some worry. He wouldn't agree to my sleeping alone in a hut because he was convinced I'd get scared at the multitude of strange noises in the night. On the other hand he privately thought I'd be offended if he suggested I share a hut with two or three burly bush-Negro men, so he didn't even suggest it to me. In fact the bush-Negroes, few of whom spoke English, were the finest examples of perfect gentlemen that I've ever met before or since, combining a delightfully humorous friendliness with old-world courtesy and a sincere concern for my welfare.

And John certainly wasn't going to suggest I shared his own hut, having already noted the bush-Negroes' knowing expressions when without prior warning he returned to the island with a strange white girl he'd found in town. With affectionate understanding, the men decided he was suffering the pangs of loneliness, and just smiled when John explained furiously that he hated having me there but had to put up with it for the sake of publicity for the project.

There was one other woman on the island at that time, the wife of one of the bush-Negroes who had come on a visit for a few days with her baby. John asked this family to share their hut with me, one that was placed discreetly away from the other lines of huts, alongside and overhung by the still-green jungle at the edge of the clearing. The occupants of this particular hut may have gained a measure of privacy from the rest of the camp personnel, but the siting of it made it the front-line target for anything that crept, crawled or slithered out of the jungle.

The married couple seemed rather proud to be singled out from the others to accommodate me, but without a single word of a common language between us we could only gesture and repeatedly smile broadly at each other as we prepared for the night and retired to our hammocks. As they were both amply-proportioned, I was quietly awed to observe them both

29

sharing one hammock, and baby came too.

My own hammock was slung at the other end of the small open-sided hut. The fleas nearly demolished me that first night. Their attentions, combined with my over-tiredness and the unfamiliarity of sleeping in a hammock, kept me awake for several hours, but then I fell into an exhausted sleep.

Some time before dawn I became hazily aware of a commotion around me, the bush-Negro woman giving a strange yodelling cry of alarm, muffled curses and my hammock swaying as people stumbled against it. I was too tired to care and stayed firmly asleep. In the morning I went into the kitchen hut, sank down on a home-made wooden bench and stared mournfully at the large plate of rice and pigs' tails Atimo put in front of me. I stifled a yawn.

'What was all the fuss last night?' I sleepily asked John.

His face showed slight embarrassment. 'I didn't think you'd heard it, so I wasn't going to say anything—though I can't imagine how you could go on sleeping with six of us falling around in the dark trying to catch a snake under your hammock.'

Some of my sleepiness fell away. 'What species?' I asked with interest.

John's mouth remained open. Whatever he'd expected me to say, it wasn't this. As yet he didn't know that snakes were a particular interest of mine.

'An emerald boa,' he said at last.

'Could I see it?'

Giving me a curious look he lifted a canvas bag down from the wall and took out a four-foot-long snake. It was brilliantly coloured, with a bright yellow belly and a green back patterned with snow-white markings.

'Pretty,' I remarked.

Dangling the snake in one hand, John scratched his head with the other.

'To think I swore everyone to secrecy because I thought you'd have the screaming jeebies if you knew there'd been a snake under your hammock the first night,' he said ruefully. 'And when I saw you totter out of your hut this morning I was even more sure of it.'

30

I stroked the boa's smooth skin with my finger. 'It's not the snakes that worry me.'

'What's the problem, then?' he persisted, observing my weary face.

'Fleas,' I said shortly.

John's attitude seemed to be that as I liked snakes he was prepared to overlook the lamentable fact that I was a woman. But I fell again in his estimation when he introduced me to his pet tarantula. I watched the hairy monster with distaste as John put a couple of flies into its glass jar. The spider turned slowly and rose into a striking position with its furry front legs raised high. When it finally pounced the movement was too fast for the eye to follow.

'How anyone can keep a thing like that for a pet, I just don't know,' I said in horror. Within a few weeks, I was doing exactly the same thing myself.

During the first day's hunting John kept me close to him.

'Although I value publicity for the project, *English girl journalist eaten by jaguar* as a headline is not the type of thing I have in mind,' he observed.

Knowing that John was likely to throw me off the island if I did anything foolhardy, I made a point of precisely following his instructions. Apparently I behaved myself so well that he decided to let me go off hunting next day with five of the bush-Negro team. He put one of them, Sime, in charge of me. After telling me that in no circumstances was I to let Sime out of my sight in case I trod on a venomous snake or got lost on one of the islands, he turned to the bush-Negro and as he didn't speak any English he told him in swift taki-taki (a kind of pigeon-Dutch, with a few other languages thrown in) to take good care of me and, whatever else he did, to bring me back alive at the end of the day. Then John set off in another boat for a different part of the lake, and the five bush-Negroes and I started off in the opposite direction. None of them spoke a word of English, but we seemed to manage well enough with mime. For the next ten hours we galloped through the islands. I watched them tracking, digging and chasing the animals. By the end of the day they had four armadillos and an opossum, and I had some good photographs and recordings of their blood-curdling hunting cries as they dashed after each stampeding animal. During all that time I followed almost on Sime's heels so that John would have no excuse for getting mad at me.

After John and I had finished our meal in the kitchen hut that evening, Sime came and spoke to him. As the conversation was in taki-taki, I couldn't follow it, but John's reply included the words 'Stay there'.

'Sty dere,' Sime repeated thoughtfully.

'Is anything wrong?' I asked John.

He looked puzzled. 'I don't know exactly. Sime says that if he's got to take you on the islands again he has to know the English words for "stay there".'

'Sty dere,' Sime said, nodding and smiling.

'I suppose I'd better find out why,' John said, and turning to Sime he asked a question in taki-taki. Sime responded with a flood of words, gesticulating arms and frequent exasperated glances in my direction. John soon began to chuckle, and by the end of the story he was rolling around and almost howling with laughter. By then a large crowd of the bush-Negroes had gathered round the hut, and soon they were hooting, cheering and wiping the tears of laughter from their eyes. Sime, meanwhile, shuffled his bare feet in the dust and looked discomfited. As I hadn't understood a word of it, I was feeling a bit left out.

'What's the big joke, then?' I asked John.

'I couldn't *possibly* tell you!' John spluttered.

After a good deal of persuasion he at last relented.

'When you were out with Sime you wouldn't let him out of your sight.'

'But that's what you told me to do,' I protested.

'I know, but there's something neither of us thought about.'

Early in the day, when we reached the first island, Sime wanted to 'go piss', as he himself put it. He went discreetly behind a tree, but I came too, so he decided to wait until later. After a couple of hours, with me following obediently on his heels, he wanted to '*go piss real bad*', and came to the conclusion that he would have to lose me temporarily in the forest; he would soon find me again afterwards. So he started to walk very quickly, in and out of the trees and round the bushes, but when he looked back I was still right behind him.

32

Then he started to run, and when he glanced over his shoulder he found me running, too. He broke into a flat-out gallop, twisting and turning through the dim forest until he could run no more. He drew to a halt, panting heavily. There was no sign of me and apart from his heavy breathing there was silence.

In an ecstasy of relief he began to unbutton his trousers. But no sooner had he undone the first button than I charged round a bend in the track, clutching the tape-recorder to my chest and gasping for breath. With the perspiration streaming down my face, I skidded to a stop beside him and gave a broad smile to reassure him that I hadn't got lost. Limpet-like, I stuck so close to him that he was in agony by the time we returned to camp in the afternoon.

'So you tell me, Boss,' he concluded his plea to John, 'how to make her stay one place tomorrow so I no go die wanting piss too much!'

And I'd thought Sime was chasing a particularly elusive animal and, determined to record the moment of capture, had broken several Olympic records in a desperate attempt to keep up with him.

3

The Rescue of
the Animals

TREE PORCUPINE

For anyone scared of animals or creepy-crawlies, or worried at the thought of sudden death, I can imagine that the jungle would be the worst kind of nightmare. If I had ever started to worry about things, if I had dreaded the possibility of coming to a sudden end as I plunged into a tricky situation, or if I'd begun to wonder in the night whether one of the many small noises was a venomous snake sliding purpose-fully towards me, it would have been the beginning of the end. The night was always full of a million sounds; if I had listened to them with fear instead of pleasure I would soon have suffered a nervous breakdown.

I was lucky in that I went there determined to like the jungle at all costs. This enabled me to accept many aspects of jungle-living more easily than if I had gone prepared only to tolerate it. Even so the first two or three days a person spends in the jungle provides quite a substantial shock to the system, both mentally and physically. Once over this first hurdle, one enters an easier period when most of the stresses seem to disappear for a few weeks. But soon or later the conflict reappears, in a stronger and more serious form. Again and again I have experienced and seen the deep psychological effect the jungle has on the people who try to live there.

The aspect I like best about the jungle is the atmosphere of bustle and drama that all the creatures give as they live out their lives, sometimes long and sometimes sadly brief, in the particular niche they occupy in the great forest. Combined with this is an overwhelming sense of variety. The insects and plants, in particular, fill one with awe; a seemingly endless procession of astonishing shapes and brilliant colours, some incredibly ugly and others that are breathtakingly beautiful. Nothing has the temerity to be ordinary or dull.

When I was out on the islands with the bush-Negroes I would sometimes disappear in the middle of a chase. When they returned to find me after the capture of the animal, they would be mystified when they saw the odd things that had tempted me to stray from them: a huge black and purple butterfly hovering above a spray of wild orchids; a nestful of baby praying mantises striking devout attitudes in the palm of my hand; a minute humming-bird, with wings blurring as they vibrated at speed, feeding from a cascade of outrageously scarlet flowers. How could anyone ever confess to being *bored* in the jungle?

The captured animals were a source of great interest to me. I had kept various tropical animals as pets at various times, but these were the first truly wild animals I had had any dealings with. The rescue-project was humane but unsentimental, a combination which in any situation ensures that the animals have the best possible treatment. But if ever there was a time when communication with words could have helped the animals, this was it. Even the most unsentimental among us was distressed by the fact that the animals didn't understand that John and his team were trying to help them. Already scared and unhappy because the rising water had trapped them on small islands, and sometimes suffering the first effects of hunger, they were suddenly faced with being tracked down by a pack of yelling dogs, forcible if gentle capture by human hands, temporary confinement in canvas bags during the boat journey back to camp, overnight caging, and for the fit and healthy another boat journey to the mainland the next morning.

Their initial terror when being hunted and caught, coming on top of weeks of growing fear as their world shrank, was pitiful to see. They couldn't, of course, understand that only in this way could their lives be saved, nor that they would be given their freedom again as soon as possible, usually within only a few hours.

Any animal that was too young to fend for itself, or that was suffering from the effects of extreme hunger, was kept in camp until it was fit for release. There were several such animals, including a baby jaguar, when I arrived in camp, and almost invariably these soon accepted captivity with equanimity, although John usually avoided allowing them to become too tame as otherwise they could later prove a nuisance to other people when they were released.

But the blind, unreasoning fear of capture of most of the animals was a constant daily occurrence. Just occasionally there was a willing surrender, such as a couple of days after my arrival when John found two abandoned owlets in a hollow tree. They were spectacled owls, with huge yellow eyes and black highwaymen's masks across their fluffy white faces.

John reached up and took out an owlet in each hand. They twisted their heads and gazed at him with composure, and then gaped open their beaks asking for food. Their parents had stayed as long as they could, but when the last foot of dry land had disappeared under the water they had deserted the babies and flown off to the mainland. John handed them over to me and for the next six weeks I regularly stuffed them with strips of piranha that the bush-Negroes caught for me.

But at the other end of the scale, and a constant worry to John, were the temperamental brocket deer. They were shy, timid creatures that wandered the forest in twos and threes. Even their capture presented problems, because they ignored all traps and could easily out-run a man. Using twenty or so men to corner a deer was no answer, either, as the animal's bones were very delicate and its attempt to charge through the throng could well result in its being injured in the mêlée.

John soon found the answer to capturing the deer without injury. The two Hindustanis were sent on to an island with their packs of dogs, while half-a-dozen boats and their occupants were positioned strategically around the island, a couple of hundred yards off-shore and hidden in the mass of dead tree-tops. The dogs milled around until they picked up the scent of a deer, then they chased it full-tilt. The deer usually circled the island once and then plunged into the water and started swimming, with a leading hound close behind no longer chivvying it but occasionally yelping to let everyone know where the deer was heading.

Meanwhile a series of hunting cries from the Hindustanis on the island kept the occupants of the boats informed of the progress of the chase. As soon as the deer hit the water, still unseen by us, a yodelling cry from the Hindustanis would be instantly followed by the sound of several outboard motors roaring into life as the nearest boats charged quickly to the estimated position of the deer. As soon as it was sighted, the bush-Negroes plunged over the side into the water and supported the deer before it weakened and sank.

The animal then had its legs bound with plaited nylon stockings and was lifted into one of the boats. This method of rescue ensured that the deer was not injured, although the men quite often suffered a kick in the stomach from a sharp hoof.

But the fear of every deer was terrible to see, and its cries of terror, particularly when human hands first fastened around its neck to support it in the water, were almost spine-chilling; this was the moment when, quite logically, the animal thought it was going to be killed. The cries gradually faded as the deer rapidly went into a semi-coma induced by shock, and as a result they were always dispatched immediately to the mainland for release, instead of being kept in camp overnight like the other species of animals. Even then, as the mainland was frequently twenty or thirty miles away from the point of capture, the deer was sometimes in such a deep state of shock that it would need repeated dousings with cold water to revive it before release. Then, as the deer staggered around drunkenly, someone stayed with it for an hour or so lest some prowling predator should take advantage of its temporary weakness to attack it.

I remember that when I returned to London some weeks later I told the BBC producer and some technicians the method used to catch the deer and then I played back a recording I'd made of one such chase while crouched in one of the waiting boats. As I turned on the recording, we could hear the distant cries of the Hindustanis on the island and quiet whispers from John as he translated their meaning.

Suddenly John shouts, 'Go, go, go!' Our outboard fires and rises to a deep-throated roar as we charge the thickets separating us from the island. The sound of the engine screams and whines as we plunge over half-submerged logs, and branches whip noisily as the boat crashes through them. A creak and crack as a dead tree topples behind us, a painful-bedlam of noise, protesting wood, surging water, straining engine.

Then a penetrating shout from a bush-Negro as he sights the deer and suddenly a blessed lull as the outboard motor dwindles and dies. The splash of water as men jump overboard. A tense moment of silence. And then a doe screams, her voice shrill with fear, sinking to a terrible and almost human groan. Again she cries above the sound of the men's shouts as they try to hold her, her voice a broken bleat sobbing with desperation.

A long silence now, except for the splashing of water as the men bind her legs loosely. But when she is pulled into the boat, the deer raises her voice one last time, a soft moan of terror that fades to a whimper as she loses consciousness from shock.

The recording ended and was followed by complete silence in the room at Broadcasting House. Then, slowly and with one accord, handkerchiefs appeared and everybody quietly blew his nose. Somehow that two-minute recording struck right to the heart of the meaning of Operation Gwamba. John and his team had to catch animals, or leave them on the islands to starve and drown. But the brocket deer couldn't understand this.

The other animals took their release with widely varying reactions. Almost none of them left their small collapsible cages immediately the door was opened. There would be a few moments' inactivity while the animal looked suspiciously at the open door, not really understanding it was free again. Sometimes we had to use gentle persuasion to get them out of the cages, rapping on the roof or rocking the cage. Once outside, though, their different temperaments were displayed to the full. I wrote the following description when returning to camp in a boat after first seeing the magical moment when the animals were given their freedom in the mainland forest:

'The armadillos rushed blindly away into the undergrowth. A tree porcupine walked slowly out of his cage and up the nearest tree, pausing to shake the spray from his rain-soaked quills. Some tiny squirrel-monkeys scampered into the lower branches, then sat looking around with puzzled eyes and shrilling with birdlike voices. And a small opossum wandered out of his cage to the foot of the nearest tree and, with remarkable trust, curled into a ball and went to sleep.'

A few days after I arrived the team caught their 5,000th animal, which officially made it the biggest-ever wildlife rescue. As it happened, this animal was a comparatively rare one, a giant armadillo whose weight was almost sinking the boat which brought it back to camp in the late afternoon. It moved with the ponderous battering strength of a tank, and after it had demolished first a cage and then the one-inch-boarded supply hut simply by walking slowly through their sides, John gave up the attempt to keep it in camp for the night and sent a small group of men to release it immediately on the mainland.

The bush-Negroes knew the meaning of the 5,000th animal; they understood that they'd achieved a world record—a great mystifying world that none of them had ever seen—and the drums began to beat as soon as the boat brought the giant armadillo in. The celebrations continued all that night, dancing, singing, drumming; the music had nothing to do with South America; these were primitive traditional dances of West Africa from where, generations before, these people had been brought in shiploads as slaves.

The island resounded with laughter and music, hour after hour. I went to my hammock about two o'clock in the morning, and lay there listening to them. Above the pulsing chorus of the night insects the drums beat in an exciting and compelling rhythm. The hammock swayed gently and a lizard rustled amongst the palm thatch. At the edge of the compound the baby jaguar, kept wakeful by the sound of the drums, snarled bad-temperedly.

Gradually the music faded as one by one the bush-Negroes fell asleep, exhausted by their abandoned dancing. By four o'clock the camp was silent with the usual pre-dawn hush.

4

Hope Joins the Camp

I had been on the island a week when John announced that he'd agreed to another girl, a TV producer, coming to join us for several weeks. My first reaction was amusement.

'What's so funny?' John asked patiently.

'A few days ago you wouldn't have even one of us on the island, but now you can hardly wait to get more of us.'

'Seeing as how I got landed with one girl,' John replied with dignity, 'I thought I might as well have two while I'm about it. Then I can resign as nursemaid and the two of you can look after each other.'

'Thank you very much,' I said.

'Oh, well,' he said grudgingly, 'you haven't been as bad as I expected. I dare say I can put up with another one.'

It was a view that he was to regret volubly many times during the following weeks. I had so far used passive resistance to counter his efforts to 'put me in my place,' but when reinforcements arrived in the shape of a blue-eyed blonde from New York we took the island by storm in a hilarious battle of the sexes: forty-two men versus two women.

I'd begun to settle down quite well on the island, but when John told me he planned to spend a couple of nights in Paramaribo at the weekend so that he could simultaneously give himself a rare rest, pick up new supplies and collect Hope Ryden and her two cameramen to bring them out to the island, and that he was letting most of the bush-Negroes go back to their villages for the weekend and so therefore I had better go into town with John, he smiled at the blissful expression that crept over my face.

'Showers!' I murmured. 'Ice-cold drinks! Real food! No fleas!'

'I thought you liked our little old jungle island,' he said drily.

'It has certain minor disadvantages,' I conceded. 'But don't panic, I'll be coming back here with you.'

'I was afraid of that,' John sighed.

We travelled back to town on Saturday, after a ten-day session on the island. I moved into a cheaper, but very lively, hotel called the Palace, at that time owned by a Chinese called Iwan, a man of great charm.

Iwan was a perfect host, always giving me a great welcome

whenever I returned from the interior, but he was also a good businessman. Each time I arrived back from the island, scratching furiously at the flea-bites under my stained and creased clothes, my legs caked with mud from the lake shore, my face blistered and gritty with red dust, and my hair tied back with a torn and dirty scarf, Iwan would materialise in the foyer of the hotel apparently out of nowhere, smoothly, unhurriedly and unfailingly.

'Christine!' he'd cry with genuine pleasure, his handsome face smiling broadly. 'How nice to see you back here safely again!'

And without even flinching he would shake me warmly by my filthy hand. Talking with great friendliness, he would take my elbow and politely but firmly steer me towards my room and out of sight of his more respectable guests in the shortest possible time without actually running.

'I'll send up a pot of tea and your suitcase immediately, and after you've ... er ... washed away the jungle dust you must come and have a drink with me and tell me all your adventures.'

Then, with a smiling half-bow, he would seemingly vanish with the ease of a genie.

The first day I moved into the Palace Hotel, I was appalled at the dirt that came off me in the shower; my brown skin was not, as I had thought, all sun-tan. I stood and let gallons and gallons of fresh, cool water cascade over me. Then I took soap, shampoo and a scrubbing brush and set to work. Soon my skin was tingling. As the grime fell away I discovered a number of scratches and imbedded thorns that I'd known nothing about until then.

Then I threw my pile of bush-clothes under the shower and washed them thoroughly with detergent. After I'd hung them over the rails to dry, I towelled my long wet hair and put on a dress for the first time in ten days. Never normally a particularly feminine woman, reaction to the rough conditions on the lake suddenly made me appreciate all the little feminine niceties so beloved of many other women.

So I brushed my hair until it shone and then pinned it up smoothly in a French pleat. My nose was blistered by the sun, but I detracted attention from it with careful use of make-up.

It was as I was intently applying mascara and eye-shadow that it suddenly seemed hilariously funny to me; how could a four-hour journey make such a drastic difference to the way people lived? If I was content enough to be a grimy, disreputable bush-whacker when out in the jungle, then why was it so important to me to feel clean and feminine when I went down to the bar among civilised people?

But I decided to indulge my sudden whim for luxury, hand-cream, nail-varnish, perfume, the lot. I was to find over the following years that this sudden hankering for femininity always occurred whenever I returned to town from the jungle, although in England my usual garb is slacks and old pullover and the minimum of make-up.

When I finally went downstairs early in the evening, Mr Sweig, the American who'd been on my flight, was there and at his invitation I joined him for dinner. The people of Paramaribo, I soon discovered, were marvellously friendly and hospitable. Whenever we came back to town for a day or two I seldom spent any time alone, for there were many invitations to lunch, dinner and even breakfast, parties and such outings as visiting an Amerindian village, seeing over an oil-prospecting ship and a conducted tour of Mr Sweig's shrimp-processing factory. On one occasion a Texan called Roy Cole from the oil-prospecting ship was so horrified when he heard that I was working out on Operation Gwamba's island that he insisted on giving me one of a set of hunting knives that had been made specially for him when he was a boy. It was a beautiful knife with a six-inch gleaming blade and an ebony handle. Roy felt that if I had that knife I would be safe from just about every danger the jungle could produce. John was humorously derisive when I showed it to him.

'What you going to kill with that?' he grinned. 'The fleas? Or maybe if a bushmaster strikes at you, you'll be able to chop its head off?'

But in fact that knife has been my constant companion whenever I have been in the jungle, and has proved its worth in an unimaginable variety of ways, such as chopping up food, cleaning fish, skinning dead snakes and cutting myself free from razor-grass. It has become a sort of talisman for me, and as soon as I hitch on my knife-belt I feel ready for anything the jungle may produce.

I didn't see anything of John the following day until I came down to a meal early in the evening, and he introduced me to Hope Ryden and her two cameramen, Sid and Abbott, who had arrived from New York late the night before and who were staying at the Torarica.

As I shook hands with Hope, my initial reaction was that never in a hundred years would she be able to take the rough conditions out on the lake. She was so feminine and ultra-civilised. She wore an expensive and sophisticated dress, her blonde hair hung smoothly to her shoulders and her large baby-blue eyes were in contrast with her briskly efficient manner. This was a woman used to authority, and she was obviously ready to get cracking and put the jungle in its proper place. What, I wondered quietly, was the jungle going to do to her? An irresistible force meeting an immovable object. . . .

The following morning we all set off for the island. Sid and Abbott rode in the back of the truck among the supplies, all words of protest stifled by the overwhelming jolting they suffered. Hope and I squeezed into the cab with John. Each time we hit a really large rut at high-speed and took to the air for a couple of yards before the wheels crashed back on to the dirt-track we leaned out of the window and looked back to make sure the two cameramen were still with us.

When we reached the dam two hours later Sid and Abbott climbed down stiffly, rubbing their rear portions in dazed silence. They already had grave doubts on their wisdom in accepting this assignment. Hope's air of efficiency hadn't diminished a fraction. After the long road journey she still looked like a film star on vacation, while I was already covered with a fine red dust that had turned to mud on my perspiring face. Only a slight wobble as she stepped into the canoe re-vealed that Hope was as inexperienced with small boats as I had been twelve days before.

The tough rescue-work resumed as soon as we arrived back on the island. Hope worked hard on her film and I worked hard on my programme, and yet through it all ran hilarity, practical jokes, and a determined fight to prove the supremacy of the female over the male.

45

A couple of days after Hope arrived, she came hot-foot to tell me something she's just discovered from John.

'Chris, do you know how old John is?'

'No.' I considered it absently, thinking of his air of command and authority, the responsibility he bore. 'About thirty or thirty-five, I suppose.'

'That's what I thought. He's only twenty-four!'

We looked at each other incredulously. Hope was about my own age, approaching thirty.

'Why, he's only a *baby*!' we both said together.

A very big baby, to be sure, but with one accord we both began to act in a motherly fashion towards him. Whenever he got mad at us about something, we would show an attitude of 'there, there, little boys mustn't have tantrums'. He retaliated by calling us the 'little old ladies'.

He listened astonished while Hope and I counted up the sadly-lacking calories in his food and set about altering a diet he was quite content with, and watched blankly when we put some wild flowers in a jam jar on the rough-hewn table for dinner-time. He would put up with it good-naturedly until he got tired of an orchid trailing in his plate of rice and then he would get up silently and dump the flowers on a side bench. Equally determined, Hope and I would get up and put the flowers back on the table, saying firmly, 'We may be a disreputable, hard-living and blasphemous lot, but we must try to retain just a *little* bit of civilised life.'

Hope now shared my hut with me instead of the bush-Negro family. She'd only been on the island a couple of days when we had a night visit from a puma. This big cat had come around a couple of times during my first ten days, swimming over from other islands to steal the few chickens John kept around camp. I've no idea why the piranha never attacked it. Apart from steadily decreasing the numbers of chickens the puma caused no trouble, and as I've never heard an authentic account of one attacking a human without provocation I never worried much about its prowling around in the undergrowth at the edge of the compound.

But the night it came after Hope arrived, we'd run out of chickens, and in its search for food we weren't at all sure whether it would choose a dog or one of us. John hung around outside our hut for a while, unhappy because we refused to have his Smith and Wesson revolver. Hope had never used a gun before, and while I had used a shot-gun and had allowed John to teach me how to use the revolver, I'd found a few nights before that it was unwise for me to have a firearm within reach when I was asleep: my reactions were too instinctive. Deeply asleep, I heard a noise and found myself sitting up and pointing the revolver, with the safety catch off, directly at the bush-Negro in the next hammock whose snores had jerked me awake. The thought that I might have pulled the trigger before I was fully awake frightened the life out of me and I refused to have the revolver again.

Hope's manner was very casual as John sat guarding us from the puma who was waiting somewhere in the undergrowth that grew alongside our hut. But when the puma seemed to go away at last, and John went off to his own hut, she admitted she was scared. Nothing would have made her admit that to John, though.

'I don't think the puma will bother us,' I said doubtfully.

Hope wasn't so sure, so with drooping eyes I obligingly stayed awake to keep her company. Sure enough, half an hour later, the puma came back. There was seldom any direct evidence of it, for it kept well-hidden in the undergrowth, but an occasional soft snarl told us it was there. Even more disturbing was the uncanny pool of silence from the night creatures that surrounded the puma like an aura wherever it moved.

As we lay sleepless in our hammocks, I had a sudden good idea, so beloved of the English in times of stress.

'I know!' I said cheerfully. 'I'll go and make us a nice cup of tea!'

Hope looked at me with an astonished face. Then she leapt into action as I climbed out of my hammock.

'Well, you're not leaving me here alone with the puma!' she said indignantly. 'I'll come and help you.'

Taking torches and my knife we crept through the sleeping camp to the kitchen hut. The camp mascot dog, Gwamba-doggo, who always slept there, lavished affection on us. He could smell the puma around camp and was none too happy at being on his own. His fat black body writhed as his tail

47

wagged and he whined a welcome. I lit a Primus and boiled water in a billy, throwing in a generous handful of tea. I added milk and sugar, collected a couple of tin mugs and we left quietly to go back to our own hut on the edge of the forest. When Gwamba-doggo started to follow us, I whispered fiercely at him and he slunk back to the kitchen. Hope objected, but I told her truthfully that John would be furious if he discovered we'd got a dog in our hut when there was a puma around, as it was unnecessarily putting ourselves into danger. Pumas were very fond of dog-flesh and would probably slash out at anything else near when they tried to take one. Hope went back into the kitchen hut, apologised nicely to Gwamba-doggo, patted him and told him to stay there. Then we crossed camp, drank our tea and retired to our hammocks.

The puma seemed to have gone. The insects and frogs were in full chorus again and we settled down to sleep. We had removed the mosquito-nets from our hammocks, preferring the attentions of biting insects to the thought of being trapped in its folds if a puma came charging in. We each had a torch in our hammocks and in addition I had my sheathed knife just in case of any trouble.

We were just dozing off when we heard the sound of heavy paws racing across the compound. We both sat up in a hurry and in the dim starlight saw the shadow of a large animal heading straight at us. As it galloped into our hut, it crouched and sprang at Hope, knocking her flat in the hammock and landing on top of her.

It had all happened so fast that Hope hadn't even cried out. I picked up my torch and knife and covered the few feet separating our hammocks all in one movement, my heart thudding. The animal was at Hope's throat, I could see that even before I turned on the torch, and I raised the knife to stab it in the neck.

A shadow veering away from the hut just as it was on the point of galloping in caught my attention. It disappeared into the undergrowth; it was only a silhouette in the darkness, but it was undoubtedly a fully-grown puma. If the puma was out there, then what in heaven's name was on top of Hope in her hammock?

Still with the knife raised high, I pushed the catch of the torch and found Gwamba-doggo's fat body pinning her down. Uncertain of his reception, he whined, thumped his tail and licked Hope's white face.

'Thanks, chum,' he seemed to be saying. 'That was a near thing!'

I think it was the sound of our hysterical laughter that kept the puma away until dawn came creeping over the forest and we fell into an exhausted doze, Gwamba-doggo clutched in Hope's protective arms.

5

The Bush-Negroes

LIZARD

We fell into the habit of sitting in the kitchen hut each evening for a couple of hours after our meal, talking and telling stories. It was a time we all enjoyed. With hundreds of flying insects crashing into the Tilley lamp above our heads and falling half-stunned on to the table, and with the eerie lights of fireflies floating around and through the hut, we'd talk about the animals we'd owned, or places we had seen. Often we talked about the jungle.

'You know,' John said one evening, 'the jungle affects everyone in one way or another. It changes you after a while, or at least...' he stopped and thought for a moment. 'It's more that... whatever you were before, it makes you more so.'

The view may have been inarticulate, but as I was to realise repeatedly through the years it showed remarkable perception into human nature, particularly for someone as extroverted as John.

'If you've got a vice, the jungle will find it,' John went on. 'I mean, look at Chris—she seems to like it here and doesn't get worried about anything, but she smokes a lot more than when she came.'

It was true. Maybe, unknown to even me, there was an inner tension that was causing me to smoke an extra ten cigarettes a day.

'Fleas?' I suggested defensively.

'And Sid eats more than when he came here,' John continued, warming to his theme.

We all turned critical stares on Sid's ample proportions overflowing the narrow bench. Sid looked aggrieved.

'I won't say how it's affected Abbott,' John grinned, watching as Abbott tipped a generous tot of rum into his tin mug. Abbott turned a face of hurt innocence towards us.

'And as for me,' John reflected, 'well, I may have raised a few eyebrows in Boston in the past'—we could well believe it—'but I'm a hell of a lot wilder and crazier since I've been out here. I don't know how I'll ever fit back into civilisation.'

'What about me?' Hope asked. 'Don't I have a vice?'

'Well, I didn't really like to say,' John rubbed his ear nervously. 'Actually, it's made you bossier.'

He ducked swiftly as an orange flew over his head.

But although we were joking about it, John had recognised

the greatest danger in the jungle: its ability to find hidden weaknesses in our mentality. Excess eating, drinking and smoking, some of the examples he had pointed out, were merely outward signs of some inner stress, a weak link in the chain beginning to bear the strain. All of us, I suppose, have a weak link somewhere in our make-up, an excess of some emotion, perhaps, or an unreasonable fear, or leanings toward some vice. It's easy enough to keep them completely hidden or well under control in civilised surroundings, where every little detail, anyway, is just a pretence, where we are at great pains to present a flattering picture of ourselves to the world. But under tough jungle conditions the pretence eventually become impossible to maintain, and then the weaknesses and vices become apparent, even strengthened because of their long suppression, like impurities bubbling to the surface of a vat of boiling lead.

Certainly our greatest help in tackling the unseen stresses of the jungle was the great feeling of friendship on the island, not just amongst us five white people, but also and perhaps in particular in the attitude of the thirty-seven bush-Negroes and two Hindustanis towards us. They loved laughter, being teased and teasing us in return. Our stories of great countries over the seas never failed to fascinate them, and there was a riotous evening when John gave them a highly-biased account of the American War of Independence, with me constantly interrupting to correct his narrative. I remember the evening, also, when we tried to describe snow to them, and ice on a lake. They sat and stood in a wide circle around us, the lamp-light flickering on their intent faces. And as we explained how raindrops turned into feathery snowflakes and floated down to make a deep white carpet, the expressions on their faces were like those of children being told a fairytale, wondering but not quite believing anything so magical could be true.

The bush-Negroes were very concerned for the safety and well-being of Hope and me. Sid and Abbott were different, they were men, and if anything the bush-Negroes obtained a measure of derisive amusement from watching the two cameramen trying to cope with the jungle, although none of the men would have failed to help if Sid and Abbott were in real trouble.

But Hope and I were different, we were *muyeres*, and white *muyeres* at that, the first that most of them had ever seen. And because, although both of us were tiny and physically weak, we endured danger and discomfort just by cracking a joke, the bush-Negroes developed a deep affection and respect for us. Like an unobtrusive bodyguard, they were always there at the right moment to divert danger, to steady us in a bucking boat by reaching out a strong muscular arm, to hold back a branch bristling with thorns that might otherwise rake our faces, or to track us down when we strayed and got lost on the bush-tangled islands.

If either of us received minor injuries, an arm slashed by a whipping branch as we plunged after an animal, or a long thorn imbedded in a foot, or even a rash of insect bites, their concern and worry, if silent and undemonstrative, was apparent from one glance at their faces. They stayed close, subdued and somehow apologetic that their country had done this to us.

Although many diseases were rife on the island, including malaria, I had only one day's mild sickness while I was there, and this was due to the simple cause of insufficient sugar. I never suffer a salt-deficiency in the jungle, as so many other people do, but I was to find that if I went a day without a hefty ration of sugar, as had happened now because our supplies ran out just short of new replenishments from the mainland, I would immediately suffer a reaction of extreme weakness and profuse sweating.

I stayed in camp all that day, half-dozing in my hammock, in a daze and sweating streams. There was only one other person on the island, an old grey-haired Negro called Amelius. All through that baking hot day he hovered around me, sometimes coming to peer at me silently as I lay breathing heavily, constant rivulets of perspiration trickling down my face and arms, and sometimes sitting morosely outside my hut as if on guard. Sometimes his quiet voice saying, '*Watra, missee,*' woke me, and he would be holding out a tin mug filled with luke-warm heavily-medicated drinking water, which I would drink greedily. Afterwards the memory of his lined black face with its halo of white hair bending over me with concern was like a hazy dream. He thought I had malaria, which had

53

already put the Dutch official who'd been helping John into hospital for several weeks, and as Amelius couldn't speak English I had no way of explaining that I would be all right again as soon as John returned from the mainland with the supplies of sugar. Amelius thought my recovery was miraculous when I got back on my feet again that evening after several very sweet cups of tea. He thought it was some kind of magic brew devised by a white witch-doctor, such as the bush-Negro foreman, Wimpey, often made up for them— frequently, I might say, with astonishingly successful results.

I stayed in camp the following day to sort all my tapes and films into some kind of order, and Hope decided to do the same. Two bush-Negroes also stayed behind, and all day we heard the sound of hammering and sawing from somewhere in the middle of the island. Late in the afternoon the two bush-Negroes came and beckoned to us. We followed them, mystified, down past the animal cages, left at the jaguar pen, left again away from the edge of the lake, down a narrow newly-cut path through the luxuriant foliage and into a small sunny clearing surrounded by palms, giant ferns and wild orchids.

The bush-Negroes stopped, and with uncertain expressions of pride on their faces they indicated a contraption in the centre of the clearing, a gift for us that had taken them several hours to make. It was a large, stout wooden box made of saplings, with a hole cut in the top and a deep pit dug below.

'Oh, I say!' I exclaimed, 'what a super loo!'

Hope squealed with delight. 'No more dodging round bushes and trees trying to hide from forty-two men!' she cried. She turned to the bush-Negroes. 'Oh, you're darlings, both of you!'

The men grinned, sheepishly shuffling their bare feet in the dust, their eyes delighted, and then left quickly.

The 'Ladies' was indeed a most thoughtful gift. Not beautiful, perhaps, and certainly quite unblushingly undisguised; there was a slight problem about splinters, and one had always to check first for snakes. But against that was the sudden privacy we had obtained, as the only approach to the clearing was by the narrow path. It had been no easy matter, particularly first thing in the morning, to find a convenient

54

bush with forty-two men roaming around a small island, intent on all their chores. And the surroundings were splendid. Butterflies hovered over one's head, large green lizards, bobbing their heads, moved out for a closer view and small birds sat in rows on the palm-fronds and sang merrily.

Our washing facilities intensely irritated Hope, as they had done initially with me. Eventually she decided that, at least for one day, something must be done about it.

'I'm so dirty I don't feel human,' she complained.

Hope organised the whole thing herself, and she thought out the details with the efficiency of a business expert. We had returned earlier than usual to camp one afternoon, and she commandeered two boats and boatmen, one of whom spoke a little English. We collected buckets, towels, soap and shampoo and went down to the water's edge just as John's boat arrived back with him and the two cameramen.

'And where do you think you're going?' John demanded.

'To have a decent bath,' Hope said airily as she walked past him and climbed into one of the waiting boats.

'You're not to swim in the lake,' John began, but she flapped her hand impatiently.

'We're not going to. See you later.'

I climbed into the boat beside her and she told our boatman to get going and beckoned the other boatman to follow us in his boat.

'Where to?'

She looked around at the vast expense of the lake dotted with dead trees. 'Anywhere you like,' she said.

We motored for ten or fifteen minutes and then Hope pointed at a small forest of half-submerged trees. 'In there,' she said.

With the other boat following we turned in, and when we reached a small secluded lagoon she told the boatman to stop and tie up to one of the trees. Then she asked him to get in the other boat as it drew alongside us.

'Come back for us in half an hour,' Hope said. She pointed out the time on his watch so he'd make no mistake. 'Off you go now.' As they both stood looking doubtful, she added firmly: 'Shoo! Vamoose!'

'Piranha,' one of them said, and pointed at the lake. As if

to prove his point a piranha leapt out of the water and fell back with a small splash.

'We won't swim,' Hope promised. 'We're just going to take our clothes off and tip buckets of water over each other.'

They nodded, satisfied, and started their engine.

'Hey!' Hope called as they set off. 'Don't forget which tree you've tied us to, will you?'

She indicated several million almost identical trees surrounding us. They grinned; they knew these channels and trees as well as Hope and I knew the streets and buildings in town. Their backs were turned to us in ostentatious courtesy as they roared off at a tangent, just in case we started undressing before they were out of sight.

We stripped off and began the none-too-easy job of filling the buckets over the side and tipping cascades of water over each other. It would have helped if the boat hadn't wobbled and bucked so much with every moment. Every now and then we had to stop and bale out the boat before it sank. We had a good scrub with soap, swilled off, and then started shampooing our hair. The sight of us must have been rather extraordinary: two naked women sitting one each end of a dugout canoe in a jungle swamp, rubbing our scalps vigorously to work up a good lather.

'Of course,' Hope was saying conversationally, 'it's not quite the way my hair stylist on Fifth Avenue does it, but I guess it will do for the moment.'

We ran into trouble when we tried to rinse our hair. I leaned over the side while Hope obligingly poured buckets of water over my head. But we hadn't appreciated how incredibly soft the water was and had therefore been as liberal as usual with the shampoo. Bucketful after bucketful was thrown over me and fleets of shampoo bubbles floated on the lake for yards around us. At any moment we expected all the piranha to rise to the surface and start blowing bubbles of distress.

'I can't get it off,' Hope complained helplessly. The water around us was white with foam and she was scooping up as much soap as water with each bucketful. 'This won't do,' she said at last. 'We'll have to move the boat.'

She handed me one of the paddles, untied the boat and, still without any clothes on, we paddled across the lagoon to a clear patch of water and tied up to another tree, thankful that there were no low-flying aircraft around.

Not without considerable difficulty we at last managed to rinse the shampoo out of my hair. Then as there was still time to spare we decided to wash our clothes. We could put them on wet and let them dry in the sun. I was leaning over the side washing my trousers when I dropped the bar of soap. I made a grab for it and in the process dropped my trousers which promptly began to sink. In the ensuing scramble to save them I lost my balance and fell into the water. Cool, calm and collected, Hope caught my ankles as I disappeared overboard and hauled me back into the boat, one hand triumphantly clutching my trousers.

'That was a near thing,' I gasped. I wasn't worried about the waiting piranha, but about the ribbing I knew I'd get from the men if I returned to camp without my trousers and confessed I'd lost them overboard.

We were dressed and feeling damp but clean when we heard the boat returning for us. The bush-Negroes seemed surprised to find us tied to a tree on the opposite side of the lagoon.

'We didn't like the tree you tied us to,' Hope explained with her usual tangled logic. 'So we chose this one instead.'

It was good to feel really clean for a change, even though it was only stagnant water we'd washed in, at least there'd been plenty of it. But we never repeated the performance. It was all too complicated and time-consuming.

The time went quickly and almost without warning it was my last evening on the island. We all sat in the kitchen hut after dinner, drinking rum out of battered tin mugs and being sentimental about my departure. I was smoking one of Sid's cigars, as I'd run out of cigarettes. Suddenly I noticed John was watching me and grinning.

'What's the joke?' I asked.

'When I first saw you six weeks ago in the Torarica, I wondered how in hell you'd make out in the jungle,' he said. 'Looking at you now, I'm wondering if civilisation will agree to having you back!'

They all turned and looked at me as I lay sprawled along one of the benches on my back, relaxed after a hard day's work. My deeply-tanned skin was scratched and scarred, my clothes were beginning to fall apart at the seams, I had a mug of raw rum in one hand and a cigar in the other.

Hope began to laugh. 'I can just see you turning up at the Savoy Hotel like that,' she said.

The next morning John took me back to Paramaribo. As we climbed in the boat, the bush-Negroes gathered at the water's edge to say goodbye to me.

'Tell them I'll come back one day,' I asked John.

He translated for them and they smiled. But we all knew I'd never see this particular island again. Within about three weeks it would be under water. During my stay the rising flood had steadily encroached on the compound with each day that passed. I didn't know how to say goodbye to the bush-Negroes, but at least I could use their musical Sara-maccan greeting for the last time.

'*Awiki nou, bala?*' I called as the boat drifted away from land.

'*Awiki-i-i-i-aye, ba!*' they sang back.

'*Ah, so-o-o-o,*' I replied.

Just before the motor roared into life, the final soft phrase of the greeting drifted gently across the water, the phrase that in their language indicated the end of a thought, a day, or a life. '*Ah, w-a-a-a-a-h.*'

When we reached the dam-head I turned on top of the raw red hill to take one last look at the lake shimmering in the morning sun.

'Will you really come back?' John asked.

'One day I will. I don't know how or when.'

We stood for a few more seconds looking at the lake. I think my departure made John realise his own time in Surinam was running out, for there were only a few more months of Operation Gwamba left now. Quite soon the animals wouldn't need him any more.

'You know,' he said quietly, 'I've lived in this crazy place for nearly eighteen months now and it's hot and dirty, and you can never get anyone to do anything in a hurry, and the wet season is the closest thing to hell I've ever come across. But I'm going to miss this goddamned country when I leave it.'

That was Surinam in a nutshell. We grinned at each other.

6

Collecting a Team

When I returned to England from Surinam in August 1965, my one thought was how to get back to the tropics again. After the colour and liveliness of South America the weather seemed bleak and faces on the street looked grey and tired. But getting back to South America was easier said than done. I sold my articles about Operation Gwamba and my radio programme was broadcast and then repeated, and I gave a short talk for *Woman's Hour*. But by then newspapers and magazines were feeling the economic pinch and cut the volume of their issues. My income from writing dropped to a trickle, helped out by writing the occasional review of wildlife books for *The Times*.

For two years I waited in vain for an opportunity of going back to the jungle to present itself, as it had in 1965. I refused to be beaten; I would somehow have to make my own opportunity. The major hurdle was my inability to pay the whole cost of a jungle expedition myself. I knew that I could probably raise about £400, but as the sea-fare alone was nearly £250 this wouldn't be nearly enough to cover the cost of interior travel, food, equipment and sundry other expenses. But supposing, I began to think, a group of us joined up? The cost of hiring boats and vehicles, and the major camping equipment, would be little more than for one person. If enough of us went out, say half-a-dozen, I estimated that we could do it for £400 each, staying in South America for about three months.

Having worked for several weeks on all the costings to arrive at this estimate, I then became convinced that such a group of people should have a specific purpose for being in the jungle; I could see all sorts of stresses and disagreements flaring up between them if they had no common purpose but were just aimlessly wandering in the interior. So why not, I thought with rising excitement, something I'd dreamed of doing for years, but which I had never seriously thought I'd be able to achieve—collecting animals for zoos?

The ethics of keeping animals in captivity is an involved and delicate subject. While we all delight in seeing animals free in the wild, this life is not always the paradise it might seem to the average person. It can, in fact, be extremely harsh, and involve a life-long constant search for sufficient food for survival, so that captivity with its generous food supplies at least offers good compensation for the loss of total freedom, willingly accepted by a good proportion of animals.

Some species, however, have a mental block about captivity and quite adamantly refuse to accept it, for no clearly-apparent reason except a craving for freedom. Unless there is an important scientific reason, I feel that no further attempts should be made to keep these particular species in zoos.

This total refusal to accept captivity is demonstrated vividly by comparing the two species of sloths. The two-toed variety is a bad-tempered beast, but thrives easily in captivity. The three-toed sloth, which looks fairly similar, is gentle-natured, extremely slow-moving, and unlike its two-toed cousin it can be handled quite safely; but only in a couple of instances has it survived more than a few weeks in a cage. The fact that it eats only the leaf of one particular tree is just part of the problem, for even when this food is made available the three-toed sloth still wastes away and dies. A story told to me by the Superintendent of Georgetown Zoo in Guyana proves, at least to me, that the reason is purely psychological.

For many years Georgetown Zoo tried to keep three-toed sloths as part of the collection representative of their country's fauna. Logically they should have been successful, for they faced none of the problems of European and American zoos in coping with temperature, humidity and daily supplies of the correct food. They provided a large, airy cage and plenty of stout branches to climb, as well as fresh leaves each day from the botanical gardens that adjoined the zoo.

But the three-toed sloths weren't having any of it. They spent every waking moment in a desperately slow but determined search for an escape out of the cage, searching every nook and cranny for some weak spot that they could prise apart. They ignored the food provided for them and eventually, weakened by hunger, they died. Again and again Georgetown Zoo tried their hand with the many three-toed sloths given to them by people from the interior, but each time the animals refused to accept life in a cage and starvation, self-inflicted, claimed them.

Finally, when the latest acquisition had weakened to the verge of death, the Superintendent could stomach no more.

Vowing that he'd never accept another three-toed sloth, he carried the gentle creature out of the zoo and into the botanical gardens so that it could at least die in the freedom it had sought with such intense if slow-motion passion. He hooked it upside down on a branch and with almost no hesitation the sloth began to eat—these were the same branches that the zoo staff troubled to gather each morning and put in the sloth's cage. Far from dying or pining for the vast jungles, the sloth thrived in the botanical gardens. Instead of trying to cage them, all the new specimens that were given to the zoo were immediately released with the first one, where they formed a contented community and even began to breed regularly, despite the proximity of crowds of people visiting the gardens.

Fortunately for zoos, the single-minded three-toed sloth is an exception. The majority of species, especially if captured young, settle down well and zoos are able to get on with their important two-fold job: scientific research, covering many varied fields such as disease, breeding, diet, behaviour, and the result of this research can eventually do much to help that particular species in conservation projects in the wild; and educating and simply interesting the general public in wild-life, which (when it is remembered that mainly private donations finance such things as wildlife rescues, and that wildlife parks in Africa could hardly exist if there were no interested visitors) is such a vital factor in the survival of animals in the wild in future years.

I considered all these, and many other, aspects before I decided I could go ahead with a clear conscience in making a collection of animals for zoos. My next step was to contact half-a-dozen of the largest zoos and ask whether they were interested in obtaining any particular species for them. To my surprise and delight, the response was very good, and I received requests for several dozen animals just from those first pilot letters, ranging from such things as anaconda and ocelot, to tamanduas and tree porcupines.

Now thoroughly encouraged, I placed a small advertisement in the personal column of *The Sunday Times*:

WANT TO COLLECT ZOO ANIMALS AND ORCHIDS SOUTH

AMERICAN JUNGLE 3-4 MONTHS 1968? HAVE ABOUT £400?
WRITE BOX——

Forty or fifty replies flooded in, nearly half of them from
women. 'Jungle-fever', it seemed, was not such an unusual
thing amongst ordinary people; it lurked beneath the unlikely
exteriors of school-teachers, secretaries, businessmen, bank-
clerks, shopkeepers and many others.

My idea was that each member of the team should have
charge of one particular aspect of the work, such as animal-
care, carpentry, photography, secretarial work and veterinary
care, as well as helping generally, and I had this in mind as
well as compatibility when I formed the team. But as I was
to find out to my cost, the fact that a person could do a
particular job in civilisation did not guarantee that he could
do it under primitive tropical conditions, and a small group
of people that proved mutually amicable round a dinner table
were just as likely to fight like cat and dog when they found
themselves isolated together in the jungle. But at that stage
I was still convinced of my ability to judge character; older
and wiser now, I realise there's no way of estimating ahead
of time which people will be able to cope good-naturedly and
sensibly with the jungle. It's a case of pot-luck.

The first addition to the team was Keith Sherwood, a tall,
shy and likable boy of twenty-two from Kew. He was working as a bank clerk and hating every minute of it. Keith had
no special qualifications for the expedition, but I liked his
quiet enthusiasm and professed willingness to do any job
given him, so I joined him up as odd-job-boy, to give a hand
wherever and whenever needed.

Valerie Barr was the next to join, a red-headed Scots girl
from Reigate in Surrey. Valerie was my own age, thirty-two,
working as a secretary, and it was as secretary that she joined
the team, in charge of a mountain of details such as helping
to arrange interior travel, correspondence and cables to zoos,
booking air-freight space for animals, ordering food supplies,
negotiations with local officials, and endless other such chores
which are the bane of any kind of interior expedition, but
more so when it's a case of collecting animals. Valerie's life
in the main had been fast cars, dinner-dates and watching

63

rugby matches, but she had always had a deep interest in wildlife and was very keen to join the team.

The next two members to join the team were both from the north. Dennis Shaw was a forty-five-year-old carpenter from Birkenhead, short, stout and bearded, with a rolling gait, a ready laugh and a broad Liverpool accent. Peter Pursall came from Stoke-on-Trent. He was a metallurgist, the same age as Valerie and I. Of medium height and fair, he had a frank and rather wide-eyed expression, and was almost too English to be true. The impression was heightened when he insisted on wearing a panama hat throughout the trip, even though the jungle dust and damp steadily reduced it to a limp and battered parody of its former self. Peter's official position in the team was as photographer.

The next few months for me were very busy, contacting dozens of zoos for more orders, writing and telephoning manufacturers of equipment and medical supplies, airlines, shipping lines, travel agents, government departments in this country and South America, freight carriers, veterinary suppliers, and an endless list of people that meant most of my days were spent on the telephone or at my typewriter, and when I wasn't doing this I was visiting zoos, buying a mountain of equipment and receiving injections for tetanus, typhoid, typhus, smallpox and yellow fever.

Difficulties arose constantly, and our plans had to be adjusted several times to overcome them. We dropped the idea of making a botanical collection, deciding to concentrate entirely on the zoological collection. Some of the animals we intended to catch ourselves and others we would buy from local people in the interior and, if they were available, from animal-dealers.

Devaluation of the pound late in 1967 was almost a death-blow to our plans. Our fares to South America and almost all the equipment I was on the point of buying leapt in cost overnight. What was worse, Surinam, where we planned to spend our whole time, did not devalue their currency in line with sterling. This meant that our capital would now be worth considerably less in food and interior travel costs when we took it into Surinam.

At that time Thea Rubinstein, an English girl who lived in

Surinam and who had been a friend of John Walsh, called in to see me briefly at Cobham on a flying visit to England. She advised Guyana as a more economic country for our operations, as it was within the sterling area and their dollar had devalued in line with the pound. Also, Thea advised, Guyana was even more beautiful than its next-door neighbour, if that was possible, and travel in the interior was considerably more developed, especially by bush-aircraft and river-steamer.

It was good advice, and after hurried consultation with the team our plans were abruptly altered to allow us only ten days, as something of a short holiday, in Surinam, and from there we would travel on to Guyana where we would spend three months collecting animals.

Orders from British, American and European zoos had by now reached such a volume that I began to worry about my ability to cope with this number of animals. Of the others, only Valerie had had even the slightest experience in looking after animals, having kept a couple of cotton-top marmosets as pets. It became increasingly obvious that I needed an experienced animal-handler to help me care properly for the collection. None of the answers to my advertisement for cost-sharing partners had come from anyone with zoological or veterinary experience, so I wrote to the four who had so far joined and suggested that, as the animal-collecting side was building up so fast, it might be wise for us to take out a joint bank loan to cover the expenses of giving an experienced person a free trip in return for taking charge of the care of the animals.

This they agreed to without hesitation, and once again I placed an advertisement in *The Sunday Times*. Although there were a number of replies, few had just the right type of experience. The exception was Brian Ridout, who at twenty-two had spent seven years training as a keeper at London Zoo and had a diploma in the care and management of animals.

But when Brian came to see me, I immediately began to have doubts as to whether he could withstand the rigours of life in the tropics. Yet he was to turn out an excellent member of the team, retaining in full his enthusiasm and loyalty, handling animals with deft capability and enduring the toughest conditions of the jungle without a murmur of complaint, while his love for it steadily grew.

Yet, and I hope he'll forgive me for saying so, his appearance and manner hardly inspired confidence as a potential bushwhacker. Tall, very thin and gangling, he bore a remarkable resemblance to Roy Hudd. He wore thick-lensed and indispensable spectacles, which I knew would give him trouble in the hot and dirty conditions of the interior, both by steaming up at inopportune moments and by rubbing his skin until it was raw. Brian always looks hungry and half-starved, even just after a meal, and his natural pallor gave no indication of the stamina that would be required of him on the trip.

His manner, too, before we left England, was reserved and stiff, but I was to find that Brian always treated new acquaintances with exaggerated caution, almost like new zoological species that should be considered potentially dangerous until proved otherwise. As he unbent, however, he revealed an unsuspected and entirely delightful wit, almost always of the dead-pan variety. Brian proved to be both reliable and an excellent animal-handler, and my respect for him steadily grew. The best thing by far, however, was a strange facility we seemed to have for reading each other's mind, which meant that we were able to handle a fierce and well-armed animal jointly in perfect safety, catching, bagging and re-caging expertly, each sure of what the other person would do at a given moment. In even such a simple thing as putting an animal in a sack, one holding the animal and the other closing the neck of the bag at the precise second of release, this easy co-ordination was a great asset.

So, with many ill-founded doubts, I added Brian to the team as employed animal-man.

Everything was building up satisfactorily now. We were due to sail from Southampton on 8 June 1968, calling at Madeira and Georgetown on the way, and arriving at Paramaribo in Surinam after a twelve-day voyage. We should spend ten days camping in the interior of Surinam, and then travel overland and by coastal steamer to Guyana, where we should spend three months collecting from various areas to be decided when we got out there. Our ship home would sail on 4 October.

Devaluation had been so expensive for us that I was constantly seeking ways to stretch the capital we should have available by the time we reached South America. One lucky achievement was obtaining a number of F.O.B. Airport orders from zoos. This meant that if, for instance, we obtained a pair of ocelots early on that were required by a zoo, we could cable them and they would transfer the purchase price out to us, when we would dispatch the animals by air, with the zoo paying freight costs. If we were able to fulfil several F.O.B. orders like this, we should have sufficient money to pay the cost of bringing home quite a large collection by sea in October for zoos who preferred to have the animals actually in this country before they paid out for them. This point of F.O.B. orders was to reach crucial importance during our trip.

It was initially in order to help team funds that I thought up a second project. The big response to my first advertisement in *The Sunday Times* for cost-sharing companions made me wonder whether short camping holidays in the jungle would be popular with British tourists, especially if the overall cost was kept as low as possible by offering a package-tour. I found a financial partner and arranged two such tours to take place during our trip, in conjunction with BOAC and a firm of travel agents, which all sounds very simple and straightforward but which took months of frantic work. Each inclusive tour cost £315 for three weeks, which included the return air-fare from London to Georgetown, and I stressed that far from being luxury safaris they would be informal and on occasions rugged.

Although the team were not officially part of this particular project, the idea was for both them and me to benefit by the tours being scheduled during our animal-collecting trip—I by having the help of a couple of the team on these first, and therefore potentially tricky, tours, and by being able to use the team's base camping ground for part of each tour; and the team benefiting by the £100 I was willing to pay in return, which would help to make up for the depletion of team funds caused by devaluation.

As we were unable to start advertising the camping holidays

67

until March, we were not exactly overwhelmed with bookings, having five on the first tour and three on the second, but this response was quite satisfactory to us for such a last-minute arrangement, and at least it meant that I should have manageable numbers while I was ironing out the inevitable complications of running these tours.

My head was already beginning to spin with the complications of all the arrangements, and the schedule for the four months' trip had to be fitted together like a jig-saw puzzle. Before long it became apparent that I should have to make a flying visit back to England at my own cost mid-way through the trip in order to see to some further business and collect some unfinished equipment for the tourists.

The schedule was now planned as follows: sail from Southampton 8 June, arrive Georgetown ten days later, spending two days docked there; another twenty-four hours sailing and arrive in Paramaribo, spending ten days camping in the interior, getting acclimatised, having a holiday and catching a few animals. Then travelling overland to Guyana, deciding on the locality for a base camp, setting it up, then taking it in turns to go in twos and threes to different parts of the country to obtain animals, sending off F.O.B. orders as we obtained them so that we could keep up an in-flow of money. After six weeks in Guyana I would make my flying visit back to England, returning on 17 August with the first group of tourists and the doctor I had employed to help me generally and to give any necessary medical attention to the tourists. After spending two nights in Georgetown we should all come to the base camp for eight days, and then the tourists and I, as well as one or two members of the team if necessary, would travel on to two other localities in Guyana for another ten days. When the first group of tourists returned to England, I should have another two clear weeks to devote to animal-catching before the second group arrived on 21 September. After a week in base camp, either Keith or Peter would take charge of the tourists for two or three days while I helped to get the animals down to Georgetown and loaded on to the ship, due to sail on 4 October with Valerie, Dennis and Brian. I should then take over the rest of the tour myself, and return to England by air with the tourists on 10 October, arriving well ahead of the boat so that I could make arrangements to receive and disperse the animals.

It was a highly-complicated time-table, but on paper it seemed to work. I crossed my fingers and hoped.

By now I had purchased the bulk of the equipment, tents, camping gear and equipment for catching and caring for animals, as well as a comprehensive selection of medical and veterinary supplies. After devaluation, I tried begging and borrowing from a host of manufacturers, trying to obtain supplies free or at a reduced cost in return for testing them under rugged tropical conditions. On the whole, my efforts were not particularly successful, with a few exceptions. Perhaps this was as well, for accepting equipment on these terms can prove to be something of an embarrassment if you return and have to confess that it was no good for the job. This didn't arise, though, with the half-dozen Everest watches presented to us by Smiths Industries Ltd. The watches had already been successfully tested on expeditions to Mount Everest, and I was glad to be able to give Smiths a one-hundred per cent recommendation after we tested them in the tropics in conditions of sea and fresh water immersion, dust, damp, excessive heat, sawdust, constant vibration and knocks. My own Everest hasn't been off my wrist for the three years since I received it, not even to have the mechanism cleaned, and its time-keeping has never faltered for an instant.

Our main living-tent also proved its worth, a double-roofed Chalet Basque frame tent which cost £150. Casey's of Bristol not only allowed us a generous discount but also made many free alterations to it according to my specifications adapting it for the tropics. The Chalet Basque proved to be entirely weatherproof and very comfortable. Unfortunately the other large-frame tent, with a single instead of a double roof, that I purchased with my own funds as part of the tourist equipment, couldn't survive the heavy storms, and instead of shedding the rain as the Chalet Basque did it collected alarmingly large bulbous caches of twenty or so gallons of water, and we had repeatedly to push up on the ominous bulges to disperse the water before the cloth split. Finding the right equipment for the tropics, I have decided, can only be achieved by trial and error; come to think of it, it's the same

69

maxim I now use for choosing people for a trip into the jungle.

Tired as I was in those last few weeks, I was positive that the coming months in South America would prove to be important to me, not only because I had proved already that it was possible to make your own opportunity if no ready-made one fell in your lap, but because I was still searching for my ultimate ambition in life and I wasn't yet sure what it was, except that I felt it would have something to do with jungles and animals. My hope was that during this trip I would be able to discover where my future life lay.

The seventh member of the team, Adrian Warren, was something of a last-minute acquisition. An eighteen-year-old student studying for BSc Zoology and a former veterinary assistant, he read the first of the reports in the local press about our forthcoming trip, and with only my name and the street to guide him he had tracked me down by nine o'clock in the morning to ask if he could join the team. Adrian lived on the other side of Cobham, a short blue-eyed boy with a mass of freckles and a mop of fair curly hair. But his angelic appearance was deceptive, for he possessed an intense scientific interest in wildlife and an almost frightening single-mindedness.

Within a short time he had persuaded me to accept him into the team, for only part of the four-month trip because of his college commitments, so that he would fly out to join us on 1 July, and would fly back on 23 August. We fixed on a contribution of £250 from him for team funds, which would include his air-fare. Adrian persuaded his father to lend him the money. There's no stopping Adrian once he makes up his mind. I didn't know at that stage that, young as he was, Adrian was an exceptionally fine photographer. Only after the expedition had ended and we returned to England did I see some of the magnificent results Adrian had achieved with only one camera and a lot of patience, and I realised that here in embryo was one of the finest wildlife photographers of the near future.

After the inevitable influx of last-minute details, now, at last, everything was finished and ready. I was too tired to feel excited in the preceding days. I stumbled on to the ship in a weary daze, still worrying that I might have forgotten some vital piece of equipment or some important arrangement. But when the ship began to dip and curtsy as we drew out into Southampton Water I was gripped by that sudden surge of anticipation that is the best part of any expedition, the moment of departure, the moment it actually all begins.

'This is it,' I thought as I gripped the rail and watched the English coastline retreating; 'I'm going back to South America, as I said I would three years ago.'

7

The Voyage to Surinam

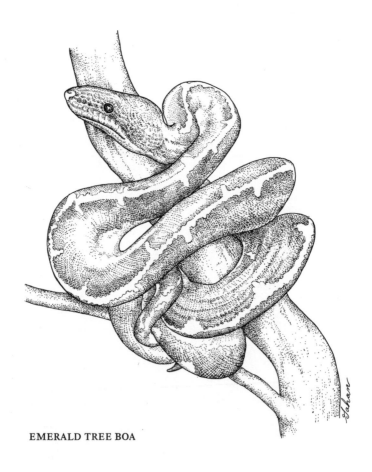

EMERALD TREE BOA

She was a beautiful ship, the *Oranje Nassau* of the Royal Netherlands Steamship Company, small but compact and very well-equipped. I fully expected to be bored by the voyage and planned to catch up on my sleep. But instead I had a wonderful holiday, swimming, dancing, playing deck games, sampling duty-free drinks and cigarettes and eating mountains of succulent Dutch food.

There was a very friendly atmosphere between the passengers, mostly Guyanese, Surinamese, Dutch and German, with just a handful of other Britons.

As Peter was working in Canada, he was travelling direct to Surinam to meet us there, and as Adrian wouldn't be flying out until 1 July, that left just five members of the team to go out on the *Oranje Nassau*: Dennis, Keith, Brian, Valerie and myself. We were placed at the First Officer's table, and after one look at Mr Beakes's stern face we imagined the idea was for him to keep a firm rein on our obviously high spirits. But his sharp wit kept breaking through his severe facade and he always led the laughter that constantly rang out from our table.

We frequently teased him with predictions of the possible misdeeds of the animals we would be bringing back on his ship. One day at lunch we explained with much exaggeration the difficulties of crating large anacondas and boa constrictors so that they couldn't escape. One or two incidents with big snakes, we admitted, were almost inevitable.

'Although actually,' Brian assured him, blinking owlishly through his spectacles, 'it would do the snakes good to have a bit of exercise along the gangways.'

'Now, all joking apart,' Mr Beakes said worriedly, 'you'll have to remember that we also have passengers.'

Brian looked round at the rest of us. 'What he means,' he explained seriously, 'is that our snakes won't go short of food.'

We docked in Madeira for a few hours and took the opportunity to go up into the hills and catch some lizards. As we had no veterinary or other documents for them, we smuggled them into the men's cabin against regulations, as animals were supposed to be confined to another part of the ship. We thought, rather naïvely, that the officers wouldn't get to hear about it.

Catching live flies for the reptiles without calling attention to ourselves wasn't easy. Brian failed to see the point of discretion and I constantly had to stop him from clambering over sun-bathing passengers on deck and dashing between the tables in the bar in his pursuit of fresh food for the first arrivals in our zoological collection.

We were seated at dinner three days after leaving Madeira, listening to one of Mr Beakes's stories, when a large fly landed on the white tablecloth beside Brian's inverted tumbler. His hand flashed out, lifted the glass fractionally and slapped it down half-an-inch to the left, his hand completing the swift circle by returning to his lap. The First Officer was still talking. Brian's action had been so split-second that it might have been unnoticed had it not been for the trapped fly buzzing furiously inside the glass.

'*Brian!*' I whispered, scandalised.

He looked sheepishly guilty and his hand crept out again and lifted the glass. The fly took off, banked once around the table and landed beside Mr Beakes's tumbler. His hand flashed out without his story faltering, up, over and down went his glass and once more the fly was trapped.

He paused long enough to smile and say cunningly: 'We mustn't let the lizards go hungry, must we?' Then he carried on with his story while the waiter almost dropped a stack of dishes when he caught sight of a fly caged inside the First Officer's tumbler.

We docked for two days in Georgetown and off-loaded the major part of our heavy equipment to await our return in ten days' time. We took the opportunity to visit Georgetown Zoo, and here Brian and I first met white-faced Saki monkeys. Before then they had only been hazy and unflattering photographs in books, for they were one of the notoriously difficult animals to keep in captivity and no English zoos had any specimens. We gazed at the Georgetown pair with something like hushed awe, completely captivated by their charm and beauty. But although we promised ourselves that we would try to obtain a pair to take back to England, I had no idea how important Sakis were to become in my life.

We were twelve hours out of Georgetown and due to dock in Paramaribo the following morning when we discovered that our complete consignment of equipment in the hold had been off-loaded in Guyana, instead of leaving on board the camping gear we would need in Surinam. Just a simple confusion over the words hall and hold had caused the mistake, but unfortunately seemed to be the start of countless other similar things going wrong during the next few weeks.

The Captain and officers were very distressed about the muddle and immediately took me down to the radio-room to send a message to their agents in Georgetown. The Captain himself spoke on the radio, but the messages were constantly interrupted by noisy atmospherics. It was a scene so far removed from my ordinary life that I was intrigued; I could easily imagine the tenseness that would fill this small room during a real emergency at sea.

At last the captain was able to arrange with the agents for them to air-freight the equipment we required to us in Paramaribo, which we optimistically thought would mean only a day or so delay for us once we reached Paramaribo.

After snatching a couple of hours' sleep I was up again to see our dawn arrival in Surinam, a memorable sight that I was able to watch from the wonderful vantage point of the bridge. It was still dark, the moon having set and the sun not yet risen. The air blew cool and moist in my face and I felt rather than saw the ship altering course to enter the wide river mouth twenty-five miles from Paramaribo. I sipped a mug of hot coffee and watched the sky grow fractionally lighter. The world was a deep dusky violet, the sky in the east streaked with orange and yellow, the colours constantly merging and changing. An early glow developed over the river and we could see a dugout canoe gliding quietly along one of the shadowy jungle-clad banks on either side of us.

The pilot came aboard, his dimly-seen figure climbing the side of the ship and taking his place on the bridge beside the First Officer. The Captain materialised and came to stand beside me, but none of us talked much; the hush of the breathtaking tropical dawn seemed to affect everyone.

Patches of thick white mist sat low on the wide river and the ship's horn blasted a warning beside me each time we ran into them, echoing with an eerie hollow note. A bank of fleecy clouds high in the east caught the first rays of the hidden sun, flushing a pale flaming-pink. A flight of macaws passed overhead on their way to jungle feeding-grounds. High above the lonely river a frigate bird circled.

The banked clouds began to glow and burn, and in a gliding movement that lasted only a few seconds the sun rose like a ball of fire above the horizon, sending long golden rays to gild the white ship and the smooth water through which we glided. With the ship's horn repeatedly announcing our arrival in long, reverberating blasts, we approached the capital city amid a strong atmosphere of coming home, a Dutch ship voyaging from Holland to an old Dutch outpost.

We found Peter by mid-day, Thea Rubinstein, the English girl who had visited me in England, having taken him under her wing. Thea also found a local tour-operator, André Mohanlahl, who would be willing to transport us and our gear into the interior in his minibus—when, of course, our lost gear reached us from Guyana.

What had seemed a simple and brief delay became far more complicated than we had anticipated. It was three days before the equipment arrived at Paramaribo Airport, and then Customs decided they wanted us to put down an astronomical deposit before they would let us bring our camping gear into the country for a few days. We didn't have much money with us in Surinam, most of it being *en route* from England to a bank in Guyana. In any case, I doubted whether we could rely on the officials paying us back the money as we left the country; repayment some time in the far future when a hundred forms in triplicate had been completed seemed far more likely.

In Guyana I was to find that Government officials in every conceivable department would bend, break and re-make rules in an enthusiastic and wide-grinned attempt to help us, but in Surinam, through two solid days of arguing in over-heated and mosquito-ridden sheds and offices, they stuck grimly and unsmilingly to the book. If one of the directors of the shipping line agents had not offered to put down the deposit, out of his own private money, we should have had no option but to go back to Guyana without our holiday in Surinam. I must express my gratitude to this director, and sincerely hope that he is still not waiting for a refund of his deposit from Customs.

We were now left with only five days to spend in the interior, and by the time our equipment was actually released to us it was already late in the day. We had to make camp well before dark, as the Chalet Basque—its one drawback—was complicated and time-consuming in erection. The three basic essentials to a camping-ground were proximity of water, sufficient flat and cleared ground for the tent erection, and being able to approach it with the minibus carrying the heavy equipment. It is surprising how few such sites exist in the jungle areas of either Surinam or Guyana. With time also severely restricting the radius of our travel that afternoon, we had little option but to travel eighty miles inland and camp by the shore of Lake Afobaka, not far from the dam-head.

Once at Afobaka we picked out a suitable flat site on the rusty-red sand dunes not far from the water, and raced against the fading light and a threatening storm to get the main tent pitched and the rest of our gear and stores under cover. The storm broke and we sat tensely watching the tent's roof. If it couldn't withstand the force of the rain now sluicing down, we were in for a damp and miserable three months. We gradually relaxed as it became obvious that the top roof—mounted on a separate frame several inches above the main roof—was coping admirably with the heavy downpour; this was undoubtedly due to the great tautness of the canvas that we could achieve on the separate frame, entirely independent of the main tent frame. It was impossible, we were to appreciate that summer, to find a more weather-proof tent than the Chalet Basque.

Three of the walls were zipped (incidentally, nylon and not metal zips are essential in the tropics, due to climate and dust, so I would advise any male would-be explorers to check the fastenings on their trousers before departure!) and could be rolled up during dry weather. One of the excellent adaptations Casey's had done for me was to fit detachable mosquito-netting walls on these three sides. This meant that in the evenings and on hot dry nights we could leave the canvas walls rolled up but still be unmolested by either snakes or the mass of flying insects.

77

We also had a small single-roofed tent for food and equipment storage, and although it was hardly weather-proof at least it kept the worst of the rain off our stores. Such things as perishables, cameras and films were kept in the main tent with us.

The Chalet was fourteen feet square by seven feet high, and provided ample space for all our camp beds and personal possessions. The fact that, men and women, we shared one large tent for sleeping went more unremarked everywhere than we expected. Certainly none of us were prepared to tolerate one of the leaky tents for the sake of modesty.

The only people who ever made any comment were some of the bush-Negroes that hung around at Afobaka, and they were simply puzzled because four men had only two women. I had soon found out on my first visit to Surinam that every *muyere* over the age of twelve was inevitably married to someone, so whenever I travelled anywhere in the interior with John Walsh the bush-Negroes always asked him if I was his wife.

'No,' he'd reply at first, offering no further explanation. This would be followed by a disbelieving silence and furtive glances. They thought he'd stolen me from someone. At last he discovered an answer that satisfied them completely. 'She's my friend's wife,' he would say easily. 'I'm just looking after her for him.'

Only Brian and I had previously handled snakes. We were not only unworried by the thought of reptilian intruders at night—unlike the rest of the team—but, as collectors, positively welcomed the idea. There was only one weak point in the tent for unauthorised entry, and that was the double overlap door of mosquito-netting. The others passed a unanimous decision that either Brian or I should sleep across the doorway to repel boarders, while the rest slept in the back of the tent where the walls were impregnable, and when it turned out that Brian occasionally sleep-walked I found myself landed with the job for the next three months. I never had to do battle with a snake at night, but many a time I woke to find an army of ants, having found a way through the door curtains, marching over me in a four-abreast column to reach our supplies of perishable food.

As fleas had been the bane of my life on my first trip to the tropics, so ants became the major irritation of my second trip. They were so darned wily and persistent there was no beating them. When we reached our base camping ground in Guyana, the ants even had the audacity to move their hills several yards closer to our food store to save themselves some foot-slogging, and one morning I walked out of the Chalet's door and promptly fell over a large ant-hill they'd built there overnight.

We tried every trick we could think of to beat them, with marked lack of success, and I'm seriously thinking of trying out a few sticks of dynamite in their ant-heaps when I next go back.

8

Hunting with Brian

The rain stopped after a late supper that first night at Afobaka, and Brian and I decided to go hunting. The others were tired, so the two of us set off alone with some catching-nets on long poles, canvas bags and a powerful torch.

It was nearly midnight and the sky was black and moonless as we padded along the dirt road that led into the forest. Some-times we walked slowly for a short way in darkness so that when we turned on the beam of the torch again any animal ahead of us would be caught in its sudden glare. We travelled a couple of miles without seeing anything and as we were by now very tired we sat down to have a short rest while we listened to the night chorus of the jungle. The cicadas were chirruping in discordant rhythm, the tree-frogs croaked in high-pitched gulps and from a mile or more away came the slow punctuating call of a huge toad like a giant with base-baritone burps.

Then we started to walk back to camp. We were rounding a slight bend in the road when I switched on the torch and saw two eyes glowing in the beam of light a hundred yards ahead. Without a word Brian and I broke into a gallop. We steadily gained on the animal, which we could now see was an opossum. As we drew near, it suddenly swerved off the road and tried to climb the twenty-foot bank to safety. Before it had managed to climb six feet Brian swooped with his long-handled net. With a snort of rage the opossum pushed its long nose under the metal rim and charged out down the bank. My own net descended on it and as it leapt into the enmeshing folds Brian dropped to his knees and grabbed it firmly by the neck. It opened its mouth, revealing a wicked-looking set of yellow teeth, and gave a blood-curdling scream more of undiluted anger than of fright.

It was a Didelphis Opossum, a common enough species, but we were particularly pleased to see that her pouch was bulging with eight well-grown youngsters, for it would be interesting to observe their progress. They have quite a reputa-tion for bad-temper, which was fully borne-out by this one as we unravelled it from the net and put it in a canvas bag.

The rest of the team were asleep when we returned, and rather than wake them we decided that the opossum would be comfortable enough in the well-ventilated bag until morning when we could build it a cage. We hung the bag on the wall of the tent and crept into our camp-beds.

When I heard Dennis moving about early next morning, I opened one eye and said sleepily: 'Dennis, could you build us a cage this morning?'

'Did you get an animal last night?' he asked incredulously.

'Not *an* animal,' Brian's deep voice corrected from underneath his blanket, *'nine* animals!'

And smug in our glow of success we both fell asleep again.

Keeping to the road during our first night's hunting proved to be a sensible precaution, for daylight revealed a terrain that would give us a broken leg or worse if we tried to travel over it at night. The sand dunes along the shore were riddled with small crevasses and rocky outcrops. The rest of the area was a mixture of steep, loose-surfaced escarpments and swampy jungle valleys without any defined trails. The exception was an area not far from camp that looked like a lush English meadow in the summertime, where the slope was gentle and the grass a luxuriant green. I know enough about South America now to bristle with suspicion whenever I see anything as attractive and innocent-looking as that hillside; a combination of attraction and innocence out there means a trap of one sort or another.

But Brian and I decided it looked good hunting country, somewhere where we could chase at top speed after any animals we flushed. We strode into the innocent-looking field and had taken about twenty steps when the long, clinging strands of grass brought us to a halt. We stared unbelievingly at the blood welling out of countless cuts on our ankles. This was the first of our many encounters with razor-grass, the greatest curse and deterrent to travel in the South American jungle, sometimes hanging in a curtain from the trees and sometimes, as now, forming a thick carpet on the ground.

We backed slowly out of the beastly stuff, using our fingertips to detach each tentacle-like strand that clung to our clothes and skin. The edges of each narrow blade, and of the triangular stem, were literally as sharp as a razor, and could inflict terrible wounds if one started struggling instead of staying still and taking time to detach each strand. The plant gave off a mild poison, which made the cuts sting furiously for the first few hours, but one thing in its favour was that razor-grass cuts always seemed to heal quickly and cleanly.

Having escaped the clutches of the razor-grass, Brian and I discussed the possibility of catching some more opossums. We thought the female's mate might be in the neighbourhood, so late that night as the others were getting ready for bed Brian and I began to collect up some catching equipment.

'You're never going out now, are you?' Valerie asked in astonishment.

'We're just going down the road to get that opossum's husband,' Brian explained.

'Be back in half an hour,' I added casually as we went out amid sundry sounds of derision and disbelief from the other four.

As we approached the point of the first capture the torch beam picked up the glow of another opossum's eyes and the following few minutes were a repeat of the events of the night before, except that this time it was Brian's net that snared the animal when we overtook it. We paused only to check that it was a male before we popped it into a bag and trotted back to camp. We arrived back only twenty minutes after our departure and strolled into the tent. Peter smiled at us over his shoulder as he spread his sleeping bag on his camp-bed.

'Change your minds, then?' he asked.

'Of course not,' I said, mildly reproving.

'We got what we went for, so we came on back,' Brian said, sounding as if we'd just slipped down to a vending machine for some cigarettes.

With great ostentation we hung the bulging sack on the wall. The other three were reading in bed, but they sat up and began to take notice.

'Ha!' Peter scoffed. 'You don't catch me like that!'

He went over to the sack and prodded it with a suspicious finger. The bulge somersaulted and gave a scream of rage and Peter hastily snatched his hand back.

'What is it?' Peter asked. His voice now held a proper respect for the two hunters in the team.

'The opossum's mate, of course,' Brian and I said together, implying that we'd ignored countless other beasts of the forest in order to get just this particular specimen. Our prestige with the team increased a hundredfold.

The joke, however, was to be on Brian and me. Daylight inspection convinced us that, far from being the Didelphis's mate, the new opossum probably wasn't even the same species. We weren't at all sure at first what it was, except that it surely couldn't be a Didelphis. He was only half the female's size, was darker in colour, and his whole construction was daintier and more attractive than the Didelphis. It was some weeks before he began to develop some markings, and then we suddenly realised that we had a young Four-eye Opossum.

The female Didelphis was one of the ugliest animals I'd ever laid eyes on. Her fur was a bedraggled grizzly brown, she had a naked, rat-like prehensile tail, hunched shoulders and a head several times too large for her body. Her snout was long and pink, her teeth crooked and dirty-looking, her eyes bulbous and mean-looking. And she smelled.

'I don't know why you bothered,' the others said unkindly when they inspected our first capture. 'Surely nobody in his right mind would buy a thing like that!'

Sadly, the Didelphis demolished her cage one night when we reached Guyana and escaped with her pouchful of babies. He departure was mourned only by Brian and me, as we intended to hand-rear a couple of the babies, thereby taming two of a reputedly untamable species, we hoped.

Dennis's carpentry, while adequate for household purposes, could only be described as optimistic by an animal collector. I have frequently found since then that people not used to wild animals always underestimate the destructive capabilities of even the smallest newly-caught animal, especially for the first few days of capture. Houdini had nothing on them. Dennis was always mortally offended if I suggested that a cage needed strengthening, and would reply: 'Nay, nowt but a tiger'll get owt o' thaaat!' I'm thankful tigers were not on our itinerary.

The two opossums were the only mammals we caught in Surinam, but we caught a good collection of birds with a mist-net, with remarkable ease once we had rigged up the net. The difficulty was in the erection each morning, for we couldn't leave it in place overnight when we knew that vampires would fly into it and demolish the fine net with their razor-sharp teeth. The two trees we had to climb to rig the net happened to be the home of hordes of small red ants with bites like red-hot needles. A very thick layer of insect-repellent helped, but more because they became glued down in the mess of grease than because it actually repelled them. But it remained a difficult and painful job each morning.

I'd brought a number of purse nets with us, as I had read many books where animal-collectors caught vast numbers of specimens by smoking out holes in trees. During three and a half months we found a total of only four tree-holes and when we netted them and smoked them out we captured nothing better than a few repulsive insects.

At Afobaka next day I had my first painful introduction to South American wasps when Brian and I were chasing a large lizard which had taken refuge in a clump of bushes. Brian circled on the outside while I crashed in to try and flush it.

Suddenly I heard Brian give a shout of warning and at the same instant I realised I was running into a small wasp-nest hanging from a bush at knee-height, the outside of it crawling thickly with small busy wasps. I couldn't help touching it as I swerved and a cloud of buzzing insects rose around me. I felt the first piercing sting on my wrist. I put my head down and charged out of the thicket like a mad rhino. Brian had very sensibly started running as soon as he had shouted a warning, but such was my speed that I easily overtook him in the first few seconds.

We two intrepid animal-catchers bolted in full flight across the sand dunes, our long-poled nets held like lances, with a thick column of furious wasps chasing after us in a dark cloud. At last we outran them. Spurred on by that one sting, I was an easy winner. The pain was excruciating, quite out of proportion to the size of the wasp, and for ten minutes I paced up and down with my teeth clenched. Then the pain disappeared and I was surprised to find no mark or swelling left on my wrist.

Brian and I explored far and wide, our enthusiasm some-times taking us to the point of exhaustion. We both had an unquenchable thirst to see what lay beyond each hill, and repeatedly encouraged each other to go 'just a bit further before we turn back'. The rest of the team weren't interested in long treks, except Keith, and in the beginning he didn't have enough stamina to keep up with us for long.

On our last day at Afobaka we all started off together for one final walk, but one by one they dropped out until even Keith had returned to camp, and once more Brian and I were trekking alone. We explored a new area to the south of the dirt-road that day, an area of mixed scrub savannah and patches of jungle. In one of the large copses we came across a delightful sunny clearing where great red boulders were tumbled around. We each chose a boulder for an armchair and sat down to have a rest.

After a few moments' silence the forest around us came to life again as the wild creatures forgot our presence. Small brilliant birds darted around and a number of lizards appeared from the crevices between the great rocks and darted over the hot ground after flies. Two black tamarins with orange-furred arms landed on a branch and stared down at us curiously. Like their cousins, marmosets, their shyness constantly battled with curiosity, but when we kept quite still they decided that we were part of the scenery. They plucked leaves and nibbled them, leapt through the dipping branches and chased each other in a grand rough-and-tumble game.

After ten minutes the spell was broken when I sneezed. The tamarins, lizards and birds disappeared in a flash and once more we were alone in the silent clearing. We left reluctantly, but it was our last day and we wanted to cover as much ground as possible. We cut across country to find the road again and before long were faced with a high stony ridge that stretched as far as we could see in either direction. We climbed to the top and saw the road far below us. The ground fell away at an acute angle and had a deep surface of loose shingle, making it impossible to descend in any normal way. We decided to scree down, although we'd never tried this method of travel before.

We threw our catching poles down first and watched them skimming at a dizzy speed, bouncing and somersaulting until they crashed against some boulders two hundred yards below where the ground levelled out. A small avalanche of shingle and small rocks followed them. Screeing didn't seem such a good idea to us suddenly, but we had to go now or risk never finding the nets again.

I crouched down on one heel and stretched my other leg out in front of me so that the heel could act as a gentle brake. 'I only hope this works,' I said mournfully, and pushed myself over the edge. Within a few yards I had reached such a momentum that I was sure I would lose my balance and plunge headlong down the slope. But I managed to keep my muscles locked in position and tried to stop thinking how many miles per hour I was doing. Brian started a second after me, but although I could hear and see the small avalanche he was throwing ahead of him away to my left, I was going too fast to risk a glance back to see how he was faring. For all I knew he was coming down on the seat of his pants.

Suddenly screeing seemed the greatest sport in the world to me; the exhilaration of our swift descent was superb. We came to the really tricky part where the gradient eased, and steered more by luck than judgement between the littered boulders and ditches before collapsing in two ungainly heaps.

We were so thrilled with our new-found sport that we would have stayed there happily screeing for the rest of the day had it not been a two-mile walk round to the head of the ridge again. We picked up our nets and discovered that it was already past lunch-time. But the road stretched invitingly away from camp. Our eyes met, we grinned slightly, and set off down the long, dusty road; lunch could wait.

We wanted to see where the road led, but mile followed mile and it seemed to lead nowhere in particular. Eventually we arrived at the side of the lake eight miles from camp, dusty, sweating, thirsty and hungry. We found nothing of spectacular interest, but even the fact that we had travelled this far in country unknown to us was a source of satisfaction.

We bathed our heat-swollen feet in the lake and then started the long walk back to camp. It was the hottest part of the afternoon, with the temperature in the shade ninety-five. Unfortunately we weren't in the shade. The sun beat down on the dusty road and rebounded into our faces, blistering our skin and straining our eyes. The road was hilly, and although we rested frequently our steps were lagging after a couple of miles.

'I wish it would rain,' I complained in a croaky voice.

Almost immediately a black cloud obscured the sun and large drops of rain began to fall. The drops increased to a downpour and we stood with our heads thrown back letting the rain wash the dust from our throats. The water sluiced over us, washing away the grime and grit and cooling our sun-smarting skins. It was glorious.

But there can be too much of a good thing. Half-an-hour later we were still trudging along through a sheet of rain, our shoes squelching, our clothes waterlogged and our eyes blinded by the stinging raindrops.

'Who,' Brian muttered reproachfully, 'wished for rain?'

'I meant just a little shower,' I said defensively.

After two hours we staggered into camp, still being battered by the storm, and with the last of our strength we unzipped the door of the Chalet Basque and fell into the tent.

'Don't bring all that water in here!' Valerie fussed, starting to mop the pools spreading around us. 'I can't think why you didn't come in when it started to rain, like we did.'

Profoundly hurt, we stood and dripped in silence. Unkindest cut of all came from Dennis.

'We ate your loonch when you didn't coom. Ants were eating it ootherwise.'

But sodden, hungry and tired as we were, and despite not making any catches, Brian and I were curiously satisfied with our last day at Afobaka.

9

A Split in the Team

HOATZIN

We travelled by coastal steamer to the Guyana border and then by car and train to Georgetown where we were generously given the use of the Scout Ground for camping while we made all the necessary but endless local arrangements for travelling into the interior. By now Adrian had arrived from England.

As we were making a collection of animals it was senseless, if not impossible, to make our base camp in the back of beyond. It had to be reasonably easily and cheaply accessible from Georgetown, there had to be a radio within reach so that we could exchange cables with zoos, and there must be regular supplies of fresh fruit and meat for the animals.

Then, with someone at base to look after the animals, we could make a series of one- and two-week forays into wilder parts of Guyana to buy and catch specimens.

While the others made a trip along the coast to photograph hoatzin birds, I went to a place called Wineperu on the Essequibo River that sounded promising for a base-camp. There was a semi-cleared site on a large jungle island three miles from the bush village, which itself possessed a store and a radio. Fresh fruit and vegetables were delivered twice a week from Bartica and we could hire boats, engines and an Amerindian boatman-guide called Vernon who knew every inch of the massive river and the thick forest that spread away from it. As I saw howler monkeys, capuchins and squirrel monkeys during my brief two-day visit, I thought we would be able to catch animals in the neighbourhood, and that groups of us might visit other parts of Guyana. Best of all, travel to Georgetown was easy and cheap: by boat or Land-rover to Bartica, twenty miles from the island, from where there were three flights weekly to Georgetown at a cost of thirty shillings a head. Or if we were carrying heavy equipment or animal-cages, we could go by coastal steamer to Georgetown docks for less than ten shillings each.

It seemed ideal and I returned to Georgetown full of enthusiasm for Wineperu. I had developed a heavy cold during my trip and in an attempt to avoid a recurrence of pleurisy, from which I'd suffered a severe attack a couple of months before, I moved into an hotel for a couple of nights.

When I rejoined the rest of the team I was worried to learn that during my absence they had set their hearts on a place called Karisparu as base camp, which I had already considered and dismissed as being unsuitable. An American diamond prospector and store-keeper, John Forbes, owned one of the few scattered settlements at Karisparu, an isolated and wild area in the low mountains, and he was very keen for us to make our base camp there, more for our company than because he expected to earn any money from it.

But the only way to reach Karisparu was by chartered five-seater bush aircraft at £50 a run and there was no radio out there, which meant no exchange of cables with zoos, and as there was no true way out on foot the lack of a radio could result in tragedy if we had an accident or anyone got snake-bitten. There were no regular supplies of vegetables, fruit or meat, and no means of local transport such as boat or Land-rover, which meant that our field of operations would be very limited. But perhaps the greatest drawback to Karisparu was that apart from costing us about £200 or more to get ourselves, our equipment and stores out there by air, and perhaps £300 to return with a collection of animals at the end of the trip, at £50 a flight we wouldn't be able to afford to send out a few animals at a time for F.O.B. dispatch to zoos in England, and income from this was vital for the team funds.

The more I considered it, the more hopeless Karisparu seemed, but Dennis, Valerie and Peter wanted to camp in the wildest part of Guyana and were adamant that the site at Wineperu was too near civilisation. Remembering that none of them had ever yet set foot in the true jungle, I tried to hold on to my patience.

I was due to leave the following morning on another two-day survey by air and Land-rover, at my own cost, to inspect some of the places to which I'd later be taking the English tourists. I was taking two American tourists along with me to oblige the Tourist Officer, Insan Ali, who himself had already helped me and the team in so many ways, and I offered to pay Valerie's expenses to come with us as we could call in at Wineperu on the way for her to have a look around. If she didn't like it, then I agreed that we could search for another site for base camp when we returned to Georgetown, just so long as it wasn't Karisparu.

Next morning we travelled by air to Bartica with Charles

91

and Beverley, the two Americans who were travelling independently of each other but who both wanted to take a brief look at the jungle. Beverley was an exceptionally frail-looking and feminine girl who had been highly indignant in Georgetown when I suggested tactfully that the trip might be too rough for her, containing as it did over a hundred miles by Land-rover over the excruciatingly bumpy jungle road from Bartica to Kangaruma.

'Honey,' she said quietly, but with a note of warning, 'if you can take it, so can I.'

In fact she turned out to be remarkably tough and unquenchably good-humoured, despite being black with bruises after our road journey; one day I'd love to have her with me on a really long jungle trek.

Cyril Sarran, who was to become a good friend and uncomplaining helper on frequent occasions, took us to Wineperu in his Land-rover, where I hired Vernon and his boat to take Valerie and the Americans on a tour of the area, and then Cyril took us on the rest of the back-breaking journey to Kangaruma where we stayed the night in the resthouse.

Early next morning our chartered Cessna aircraft arrived to pick us up at the nearby Mahdia airstrip. The attack of pleurisy that had threatened in Georgetown had now developed, and I wasn't looking forward to flying with no oxygen and when my breathing was already so restricted; but there wasn't much I could do about it and anyway, I thought with vain optimism, I could have a rest when we got back to Georgetown that evening. But my mood wasn't improved when the pilot told me he'd sub-chartered his aircraft to the rest of the team in Georgetown and had already taken Dennis and some equipment into Karisparu that morning on the way to pick us up.

We took off and, as planned, landed at the top of Kaieteur for an hour to see the magnificent falls dropping into the eight-hundred-foot gorge. Our next stop was unscheduled, as the pilot had to touch down at Karisparu a few miles away to pick up some oil he'd left there. The situation then began to get farcical. Not only did Dennis refuse my request that he come back to Georgetown with us, but also Valerie decided to stop there too, and Charles voted to stay there for one night and travel out next morning when the pilot brought in the rest of the team, as they'd arranged with him.

Beverley, who was beginning to boil over on my behalf, listened to them incredulously. She stood on the bush-strip, hands on hips, a minute but formidable mid-west school-mistress, and called to the pilot in a voice that carried clearly to the others.

'Say, you wouldn't be thinking of running out on us too, would you?' she said coldly. 'Because I don't think I could fly this crate back to Georgetown without some help.'

The pilot took Beverley and me on to Imbaimaidai, which proved impossible for future camping because of steep slopes and the bank being forty feet above the river. By the time we got back to Georgetown in the early evening, I was simultaneously laughing at Beverley's wisecracks, wheezing painfully and keeping a firm rein on my icy anger with the team.

A meeting that evening with what remained of the team, with Peter now self-appointed leader, produced no easy solution. He said flatly that they were making a base camp at Karisparu, so I would just have to accept the decision without any more arguing. I looked at him for a long moment in silence. I had repeatedly given them all my reasons for considering Karisparu dangerous, completely cut-off and without a radio, and senseless from an economical point of view. But they refused to accept my estimates on the cost of getting in and out of Karisparu, reckoning that they could do it at half the price.

There was only one thing I could do; but it still hurt. Standing up, I said: 'All right, then, you go to Karisparu and see if you can make it work. I'm withdrawing myself and my money from the team. I'll employ people in place of the team to help me set up my own camp at Wineperu.'

As I left, Peter's face was angry and astonished. He'd felt sure that their precipitate action during my absence would force me to go along with them.

With what remained of the evening I started to arrange employing a small staff to help me get animals and later look after the tourists. But next morning a very subdued Peter was back again, admitting that I'd been proved right on the air-freight costings. They'd actually taken all the team equipment and several month's stores out to the airport at dawn, ready for the Cessna to start ferrying them into Karisparu; but Peter's first sight of the tiny aeroplane caused him to make some hurried calculations. His figures stated quite plainly, as mine had done, that the cost of taking in all the team, their stores and equipment, as well as bringing out even a moderate collection of animals after three months, was way beyond the resources of the team even if I had not withdrawn just over £100 of my money the night before, as well as cancelling the arrangement to pay them a further £100 for helping with the tourists.

Peter handed the problem to me, together with his idea of a solution. If I would agree to join the team again as leader, they were willing to accept Wineperu as base-camp. But rather than waste £50 sending an aircraft in just to pick up Dennis and Valerie, wouldn't it be better for a couple of them to go out to Karisparu with the minimum of stores and equipment and for the four of them to stay there collecting for a few weeks? Then, in perhaps four or five weeks' time, they could all come out with the animals and join us at Wineperu, and those of us who had been occupied setting up the base-camp would then be free to make our own trip somewhere else to collect animals. In this way the cost of their going to Karisparu could be limited to just one more flight—the £50 that it would cost to fetch the other two back anyway—and if the animals travelled in bags instead of cages they could just about pack into two trips on the journey back in August.

I listened to Peter's proposition without much enthusiasm; it was far from ideal when compared with my original plans. But both I and the younger members of the team had been hurt by the split, and this at least offered the opportunity for us to patch things up. Perhaps it would be wise to make the best of things. The cost would be cut down by only half the team and the minimum of supplies going in.

It's easy to look back now and see that I clearly made the wrong decision; but it was a difficult choice at the time. I was particularly swayed by the removal of one of my main objections to Karisparu, its danger, when Peter told me that John Forbes had taken in new batteries for his old radio that morning. It was some weeks before I discovered that it was an aero-radio that only worked when an aeroplane was actually in the air, and John Forbes's plane was a months' old crumbled wreck at the end of the bush-strip.

And so I agreed to Peter's proposition, and let myself in for a lot more heartache and butchered plans.

All four insisted that I myself must decide which of them went where, and at this point I made a second mistake by wrongly dividing the team, although from the best intentions. If they were going to get any animals at all, I thought, Brian would have to go to Karisparu, although as we hunted so well together it was a pity that we would be separated for half our time in the country. And I thought that as Adrian would only be in Guyana for six weeks, it was only fair if he spent that time catching animals instead of slogging away building up a base-camp and only catching in spare moments. That left Peter and Keith to come to Wineperu with me. One particular asset of this arrangement was that both camps had an experienced snake-handler, which was advisable for safety if not for catching.

Before long I was to feel like kicking myself hard for making this arrangement. For by buying and by a bit of catching I was to build up a beautiful little collection at Wineperu, while their luck was almost completely out up at Karisparu and they obtained little more than a couple of dozen snakes. While I had the desperate worry at Wineperu of trying to persuade two amateurs to look after the animals properly during my absences, Brian, who had been brought to Guyana specifically to look after the animals, had only a handful to care for at Karisparu.

Thinking that everything was now on an even footing again, and blithely unaware of the difficulties we would have to face later in the summer, Peter, Keith and I took all our heavy. equipment and stores round to Bartica by steamer, transferred everything to small boats and travelled up to Wineperu. Even with a mountain of equipment, the total cost for our journey was less than £10.

We set up a good camp on Murray Island, three miles downstream from the bush village. We spent a morning clearing away the new growth and piles of dead wood from an old camping ground and then erected the Chalet Basque in the shade of a giant palm-tree, which I imagine will make a few expert campers wince. It was true that rain-drops fell from the palm-fronds on to the tent roof for a full hour after each storm, and that we had a few near-misses from sharp-edged branches breaking off in high winds, but the deep shade the tree threw over the tent throughout the day more than made up for the other inconveniences.

Like many hundred other jungle islands in the Essequibo, Murray Island was uninhabited. Apart from the camp compound it was very thickly forested—such a wilderness, in fact, that during our many weeks there we were never able to explore it fully.

During the following days we cleared a site for my own large frame tent, which we intended to use as shelter for small animal cages, and the food-store tent. Our next step was to start building some large animal pens, using a combination of wire-netting, saplings and split bamboo. Peter, without any pre-conceived notions about carpentry, proved to be an excellent cage builder, first asking me exactly what I had in mind for each new pen, size, shape, type of door and perches, and then proceeding to build a first-class and accurate job with me and Keith acting as assistants.

I had hired boats from the manager of the timber-felling concern at Wineperu, a Scotsman in his mid-thirties called Joe Young. His was a flamboyant personality which could be liked or disliked, but never ignored; at least things were never dull when he was around. He was a Scot of the traditional but rarely-encountered type, believing a woman's place to be in the kitchen and no answering back, so what did I think I was doing wandering around the jungle when I should be at home darning hubby's socks?

Life was a constant battle of wits to out-do each other and cut each other down to size, but the war was invariably conducted with humour. Joe set his mind to proving that the jungle was no place for women in general and me in particular. He was especially indignant that a woman had moved into his own large patch of jungle, which he ran as a miniature kingdom with himself as its emperor. He liked it that way and didn't want it changed, but already he was worrying that my obvious independence and wilful insubordination to him was setting a bad example to his women employees, especially Milda, a young Indian guide, and Naz, his beautiful, sloe-eyed East Indian cook.

None of his many employees seemed to notice, let alone object to, his outrageous rudeness to them, nor the brusqueness of his orders, but they were surprised and then delighted when I refused to let him bully me even in small ways.

Having organised an efficient and comfortable camp, we started to clear some further sites for the tourist tents which would be required later, and at the same time turned our attention to trying to get some animals. I hired Vernon and his boat for several days in a row so that we could have a thorough look around the area, travelling both on the river for miles in each direction, and on foot through the massive forest where we would soon have been lost without Vernon as guide.

He was an Arawak Indian, short but muscular, with a strong-featured handsome face and a ready laugh. There were times when he turned unreasonably stubborn, and times when he couldn't resist taking advantage of our indulgence. There were countless occasions when he mysteriously disappeared just as we found a job for him to do. There were times when I got mad at him, and times when he'd fling down his machete and temporarily refuse to work for me any more. But underneath it all, we liked and respected each other, and apart from these occasional moments of flaring temperament, we got on very well.

He was both expert and fearless on the river and in the forest, and I never had any hesitation in trusting my safety to him and I deferred absolutely to his judgement in any potentially dangerous situation. He in turn was vastly impressed to see me handling large snakes, and this I found very flattering.

Although Vernon was a good hunter with a bow and arrow, he had never caught animals alive; but it was actually he who caught one of our first specimens at Wineperu. It was a very hot Sunday afternoon and I had gone to explore a pond in the forest about a mile behind the village. On their way to join me, Milda and Vernon saw a small caiman, about fifteen inches long, in a creek they were passing. Vernon, who was even more agile in the water than on land, leapt into the creek and managed to get a grip on the alligator's neck as he plunged under the surface. Even so, the caiman twisted its neck and bit Vernon's thumb, but thinking how pleased I'd be if he brought me an animal, he managed to hold on and bring the caiman to shore. Then he and Milda carefully tied it up with thin vines so that they could carry it safely and set off to find me.

I was not only pleased at their catch, but overjoyed, for I could see at a glance that this was no ordinary species of caiman but something really unusual. Its skin was a reddish-brown and very heavily-armoured, the scales raised in great scollops. Most remarkable of all was its tail, which was serrated with thick, upright spikes in a way I had never seen before.

Vernon and Milda had been rather over-enthusiastic in the way they trussed the caiman around its legs and snout; even its tail was lashed down. The poor creature could hardly twitch a muscle so I took out my bush knife and began to cut it free; after all, it was too small to hurt me providing I kept my fingers away from its teeth. Only when I noticed the other two's mixture of laughter and chagrin did I realise that I was being undiplomatic, for they had just spent half-an-hour tying it up. I explained my apparent bravado by tactfully pointing out that I had a bag to put it in.

As I cut the caiman free of the last vine, holding it in the air with my hand around its neck, I was not unprepared for the lash of its tail. But I hadn't realised the significance of this new caiman having spikes on the upper part of its tail. Instead of striking sideways, the caiman lashed upwards, and the sharp prongs on its tail hit the underneath of my arm with such painful force that I nearly dropped it. That caiman was undoubtedly one of the most consistently vicious and bad-tempered creatures I've ever encountered. It was only when I returned to London with it and was able to get it properly classified that I understood the reason for it being so aggressive. Instead of its being a baby of a normal-sized species of caiman, it was a half-grown specimen—several years old—of a particularly rare species of dwarf caiman *paleosuchus trigonatus*, which is only just over a yard long when fully-grown.

Rubbing my arm ruefully, to the amusement of Milda and Vernon, I put our catch in a canvas bag and walked back with them to the village.

10

Alone on Murray Island

As well as the animals we had obtained in Surinam, the Four-eye Opossum, a number of birds, lizards and frogs, other animals were beginning to come in, but very slowly: the caiman, a small water snake Joe found in his garden, some tortoises, a fer-de-lance, more frogs and toads, and someone in Bartica gave us a baby black coatimundi he had raised on the bottle.

Local hunting was proving very difficult, partly because the heavy wet season was extended and most of the animals stayed on the high dry ground in the heart of the forest, but mainly because of our lack of good catching equipment. In the last-minute division of equipment and stores at the airport before Adrian and Brian flew to Karisparu, all the best catching poles and nets had accidentally been left in their luggage, and we found ourselves at Wineperu with only a couple of huge poles which were too unwieldy to use in the thick forest.

I was also fretting because we had no box-traps, and the tracks on our island alone proved that we could have caught a fair number of small mammals if we could have set baited traps at night. In England I had been on the point of buying several box-traps of various sizes when Dennis heard how expensive they were and insisted that he would be able to make some on the spot. So I cancelled the order for box traps, and now we were at Wineperu and Dennis was up at Karisparu.

We made a number of attempts to construct our own traps, as capuchins, howlers and squirrel monkeys were common along the edge of the river, and a pair of toucans came to feed each day from a tree only a few yards from our main tent. But our rudimentary efforts were quite unsuccessful.

One of the most frustrating things was that the harder we concentrated on hunting, the less success we had, and it was only when we weren't trying that a few specimens almost walked into our arms. One such capture was the fer-de-lance snake.

One day soon after our arrival we decided to make an all-out effort to obtain some specimens. Early in the morning Vernon took the three of us down-river and we spent several hours walking through the forest. Unfortunately for us it was one of those odd days when every living creature seemed to have disappeared off the face of the earth. We had a quick lunch back at camp, travelled up-river by boat and spent the whole afternoon walking through that section of the forest. Nothing.

We returned to camp at dusk, had supper and, determined not to be beaten, went to Wineperu, left the boat at the jetty and then hunted with torches for several miles along the lonely bush-track that led out of the village. Our luck was well and truly out and our bags were empty when we returned to Wineperu at midnight.

Rather than drag Vernon back to the island after such a hectic day, we kindly told him we'd take one of the canoes and paddle ourselves back while he went to his home in the village. Unluckily for us a storm broke just after Vernon left us and before we reached the jetty, soaking us to the skin and making it impossible for us to leave in the boat because of bad visibility. We needed a minimum of clear starlight to be able to find our way through the rocks in the river and to pick our particular island out of dozens. Over-shooting our camp in the big river, a mile wide at this point, would have dire consequences, for the current was too powerful for us to turn back against it with only paddles to assist us.

We sheltered in a leaky wooden hut for an hour while the rain lashed down, until at last the storm cleared and we were able to set off. More by luck than judgement we reached the small inlet to our camp without mishap, at two o'clock in the morning, wet, shivering, hungry, weary, scratched and scarred by the jungle, and with not even a frog to show for our efforts.

Soon after we got up next morning, Peter casually hit the trunk of the palm-tree beside the main tent with his machete as he talked to us. Dislodged by the vibration, a snake fell out of the branches and landed at his feet. I dashed forward and caught it. My whoop of joy was drowned by a howl from Peter.

'All that work yesterday,' he almost cried, 'and all we had to do was stay in camp and hit this tree!'

But the collection grew by fits and starts and suddenly flowered when, on a couple of hurried visits back to George-town to see to business, I was able to buy a number of animals. The pens gradually filled and the camp really came to life with movement, colour and noise.

There was a blue-and-gold macaw, who would sit out in the rain with outstretched wings until he was drenched; a pair of sulphur-and-white-breasted toucans, who shared a large pen with a magnificent tiger-bittern; parrots, parakeets and parrotlets; a tree-porcupine that was promptly dubbed Percy; six squirrel-monkeys and five capuchins; two more baby coatimundis; and several snakes, including a couple of boa constrictors, a ten-foot anaconda, a large emerald boa and a rainbow boa, whose burnt-orange skin literally gleamed with the colours of the rainbow when the sun caught it.

I paid for these animals with my own money and told Peter and Keith that the team as a whole, when we all joined up again, could decide whether they wanted to buy them from me at the same prices I had paid, leaving payment until the last minute if they liked. It was to prove about my most sensible action during the trip.

Although there was still plenty of work to do, Peter and Keith were beginning to get a bit restless, and I thought it would be a good idea for them to have a couple of days away from Murray Island before I had to fly back to England for a week on 10 August. They would have to be alone together on the island for ten days during my absence, and I was worried about the effect of their having ten days of each other's undiluted company. They had reached the stage, after several weeks of jungle living, where the deeper subconscious stresses begin to come to the surface. It was a lot tougher for them than for me, because I had the totally absorbing interest of the animals. The men were not animal-addicts and it was becoming increasingly obvious that their main purpose in being there was to seek adventure. Unfortunately, adventure seldom happens to order, even in the jungle, and even then it usually chooses someone who doesn't anyway ask for it.

My idea of sending them on a trip wasn't without its selfish motive as well. I could imagine nothing more desirable than being completely alone with the animals on the island for a couple of days. I had a hard job convincing Peter and Keith of this, for their initial reaction to my suggestion was that it would be unfair and unwise to leave me there alone while they both went away together. Anyone in her right mind, they said, would hate being cut off alone on a jungle island, and would certainly get scared at all the bumps and bangs, screams and squawks we always heard at night.

Actually, I was safe enough on the island for I had a paddle canoe there, and while I wouldn't be able to tackle the current up to Wineperu, if there was a real emergency and I was injured or snake-bitten, I could let the river take me three miles down-stream to where men were working a quarry carved out of the jungle bank.

Once Peter and Keith were really convinced that I didn't mind being left alone, their enthusiasm began to show through. We fixed their trip for the last weekend before I flew back to London, leaving at dawn on Saturday; their return on Monday morning would coincide with my own departure. They decided to go to Tumatumari, not far from Kangaruma, where Peter hoped to photograph a tribe of Amerindians. Transport was no problem as the weekly 'bus' —a ramshackle lorry—could both take them and deliver them back to Bartica, where they could hitch a lift back to Wineperu on one of the timber-barges.

Vernon came to fetch them very early on the Saturday morning to take them to Wineperu, from where Joe was taking them by Land-rover to the seven-mile junction to pick up the lorry. As I knew Vernon was going to Bartica that morning, I gave him some money to fetch a supply of cigarettes for me and fruit for the animals, as I was short of both. As I stood waving while their boat roared off, I had no inkling that the next two days were to be packed full of incident, and were also to contain the first tiny seed of my greatest dream.

A quiet descended over Murray Island as the sound of the outboard motor faded. The echoing calls of the toucans in the aviary, the chattering of the capuchins and the soft squeaks of the baby coatis, all stressed the peace rather than disturbed it. Before I set to work I made a cup of coffee and took a canvas chair outside in the early morning sun, settling down to enjoy a quiet half-hour of welcome solitude. I sat so quietly that the animals surrounding the compound soon forgot I was there.

Squirrel monkeys—or sakiwinkies, as they're so delightfully known in Guyana—with slim, tiny bodies and long tapering tails, forgot their bickering for once and chased flies with expressions of intense concentration on their pansy-like faces, clapping their yellow-furred arms together and looking astonished when they missed.

The tiger-bittern, a sunburst of flame-coloured feathers, strutted importantly along the ground of the aviary and pulled some fish from its bowl of water, while on a higher branch the toucans peered down their long noses and momentarily considered teasing him before relinquishing the idea and turning back to their dish of bananas, tossing the pieces to the back of their throats with a casual flick of their beaks.

The macaw croaked softly and preened his long tail, pausing to scratch his hooked beak delicately with a claw. The tree-porcupine, curled in a prickly ball, snuffled and snored in his sleep; tonight, I knew, he would keep the camp awake half the night with the noise he made gnawing, scratching, climbing and thumping, all done in ponderous fashion while his short-sighted eyes gazed solemnly over his bulbous clown's nose.

The parakeets had a hysterical squabble over a choice piece of food and the other small birds fluttered and fussed in sympathy. The boa constrictors and anaconda lay in a loosely-coiled intimate tangle, while the emerald boa and rainbow boa clung in tight complicated knots to a branch. The capuchins made a dash at a butterfly that fluttered near their pen, watched disappointed as it floated out of reach and into the forest, and then settled with complete absorption to grooming each other's fur.

A fish leapt in the river, and on the far bank, half-a-mile away, a troop of red howlers gave voice, the sun glinting on their flame-coloured fur as the eerie sound rose in waves, slowly swelling and receding, like surf on a reef, the wind over the tree-tops and rolling on muted drums, flowing and ebbing powerfully yet insubstantially, a primaeval and ghostly chorus that finally faded into nothing.

As the sun soaked into me, so did the tranquillity of being alone with my animals on the island. I think I was happier, more deeply content, at that moment than at any other time in my life.

I let the two baby brown coatimundis, Bill and Ben, out of

105

their cage and they tumbled around my feet as I prepared their raw egg and milk. I smiled as I recalled their memorable misdeed soon after I had brought them to the island. They were only a few weeks old, the size of small puppies and with much the same predilection for boisterous play. Their faces were rather fox-like, but with long rubbery noses that were used to explore thoroughly every nook and cranny and to root in the earth for grubs and insects. Their feet were equipped with curved claws for climbing and digging, and their long tails were ringed in shades of light and dark brown.

I have a great affection for coatis, even though their high intelligence and curiosity are forever leading them into mischief. They frequently make good pets, although adult male coatis are often treacherous and I know several zoo people who bear scars to show what terrible injuries adult coatis are able to inflict.

Bill and Ben, like most baby coatimundis, were quite tame from the beginning, but for safety's sake I kept them in a cage in our living tent for a couple of days after their arrival. If they wandered off into the surrounding forest I knew they would be too small and fast for us to find them again. But on the third day I thought they were tame enough for us to trust them loose in the compound while we photographed them. We stuck a large branch in the earth to simulate a tree, and let Bill and Ben loose among the leaves and twigs.

All went well for ten minutes while the coatis climbed and played. Then they climbed down to the ground and as if at a prearranged signal Ben charged north while Bill made a mad dash for the south and shot up a small tree at the edge of the clearing. Shouting to Keith to keep Ben in sight and try to hunt him back to camp, I snatched up a long-poled net and with Peter went after Bill. At least, I think it was Bill, but the brothers were so much alike that we hadn't been able to resist naming them after the Flowerpot Men—'Is it Bill—or is it Ben?'

Bill was having a hilarious time at the top of the small tree, riding the swishy sapling like a bronco-buster as it dipped under his small weight. The tree was completely surrounded by a mass of razor-grass hanging like a thick curtain, but when I saw the coati gathering himself for a leap to the next tree

106

and a direct route to the forest, I leaned against the razor-grass and swung with the long-handled net. I missed. Bill landed in the next tree and raced through the branches until in a few seconds he was out of sight.

Meanwhile I'd discovered I couldn't move. The razor-grass was wrapped around my throat and bare arms, and a thick swathe had fallen across my shoulders, cutting off my retreat. I called to Peter and he waded in and carefully cut me free. It was a delicate and time-consuming task, with both of us inevitably becoming slashed in the process, and it was over twenty minutes before I was completely freed. By then the coatis had entirely disappeared.

Dusk was fast approaching and I knew they were too small to survive a night away from camp. Vernon had found ocelot tracks on the island, and there were bound to be one or two big snakes out in that wilderness. We searched frantically for them, but it was hopeless. The forest was so big and the coatis so small; even their colouring was against us, for if they kept still close to the ground they blended so well that we could pass within a couple of yards and not see them.

In the end we had to give up. We sank exhausted into chairs outside the tent to get our breath back. The blood from the razor-grass cuts across my throat and down my arms had dried now and I looked like a victim of Jack the Ripper; Peter didn't look much better.

Suddenly we froze as Bill and Ben trotted nonchalantly out of the forest and into the clearing, squeaking to each other like children's rubber toys. They paused to push their questing noses under a log. Then they continued their brisk but unworried journey to the tent behind us where they were caged. As they trotted past our chairs we suddenly unfroze and threw ourselves headlong upon them with cries of triumph. Bill and Ben gazed at us in astonishment; they hadn't intended going anywhere except home. They'd enjoyed playing out in the forest, but now it was time for supper and a comfortable bed. After that we let them run free for most of the time and although they sometimes disappeared into the forest on their busy quest for insects, they always came back again.

Alone on the island now, I let them play around my feet as I worked. There were still a lot more cages to build, for we

107

were expecting the rest of the team from Karisparu to arrive in a fortnight's time with their animals.

After a lunch of biscuits and cheese, I had a fancy to go fishing. The island had too many underwater snags along its banks, but there was another tiny island four hundred yards away from the camp where the fishing was good. As it was almost opposite the compound, it simply meant paddling the boat at an angle through the current to get there. Two of us had frequently paddled across to do some fishing.

It was as I glided out of our inlet into the main stream that I began to suspect the wisdom of my action. For one thing, although Vernon had taught me to handle a boat well, there was quite a difference of power between one and two people. And for another, I had the biggest and most cumbersome boat, instead of the light canoe Vernon usually left with us. Worst of all, the current was particularly fast and sweeping that day.

I pointed the boat up-river to counter my drift and began to paddle with long deep strokes. That boat was a real cow for steering and within a few yards its head began to swing downstream. I fought to correct it, but in the end I had to let it swing round in a full circle before I could get it heading up-stream again.

The sun was blazing down, but I couldn't pause to rest for a second otherwise the current would take me. The swift flow of water turned the bows again, and once more I had to let the boat swing right round. I was halfway to the island now, but the current had pushed me downstream from it. Panting and sweating, the perspiration running into my eyes and half-blinding me, I tried again and again to force the boat against the river. But it was too much for me.

Fear came suddenly when I lifted my head and glanced round to pin-point my situation before I changed direction. I was out in mid-stream now, where the current ran strongest, and I was going to have my work cut out getting back to Murray Island. I was already a long way below camp, and there was just one jutting headland further downstream before the island and the current diverged in opposite directions.

I felt a sudden surge of helplessness, as if a large animal had me in its grip. I brought the boat round and threw every ounce of strength into trying to drive it across the current before my sideways drift took me past the headland, my last chance of landing. I got very close, but the water roared down here in a white torrent. Only a few yards from land, I saw that I was going to be swept past the headland.

I was close enough to risk abandoning the boat; if I dived over the side, my impetus would bring me to the bank. But the boat belonged to Joe; his jubilation at my incompetence if I lost it would be unendurable. He would have proved that the jungle was no place for a woman.

In those last seconds as I hesitated, I saw a faint chance of saving both of us. The boat, caught in the grip of the racing water, was bearing down to the point of the headland, just within reach, if I was lucky, of a slender branch that dipped towards the water where a tree leaned at an angle over the river. I dropped the paddle, wedged myself against the seat and leaned over the side of the boat. My fingers touched leaves and then curled around the slender branch. I held on. At first I thought the branch would snap as the weight of the pulling boat stretched it, and then that my arms would be pulled out of their sockets. But neither happened and inch by inch I was able to pull the boat back until I could reach another stronger branch, and then another, until suddenly the strain on my shoulders eased as we glided into a quiet inlet away from the current.

Sobbing for breath, I collapsed into the bottom of the boat, soaked with perspiration and trembling from the frenzied exertion. The mighty Essequibo, sometimes tempestuous, sometimes tranquil, but always strong; far too strong for me. I remembered a few evenings before when, in a rare moment of solemnity, we had all been discussing danger and death in the jungle and Joe had said with quiet conviction: 'The river will get me in the end.'

Oh, well, I thought, as I doused my face with cool river water, at least I hadn't lost his boat. It took me over an hour to haul it back to camp. At the end of the rainy season the water still stretched twenty feet back amongst the trees and tangled bushes, so instead of being able to walk along the bank and pull the boat with a rope, I had to stay inside it and haul it from branch to branch upstream against the current.

109

By the time I reached camp, I felt badly in need of a holiday in some quiet place, Blackpool perhaps.

Vernon didn't come back with my cigarettes and fruit. Together with Joe, Naz and Nilda, he was drifting helplessly on the river several miles downstream in the dark night, the ignition having failed on their speedboat when they were halfway back from Bartica. They drifted until dawn, longing for a stiff rum and some blankets to keep them warm.

Early next morning I fed the collection with some boiled eggs and rice and a few cans of vegetables. It was all I had until Vernon returned with the fruit supplies.

I stood watching the capuchin monkeys for a while. There were five of them in the big pen, which had a walk-in door: Kitty, a big old female; another young adult; two half-grown youngsters; and a baby, about a year old. The baby was not the offspring of either of the adults, and I was concerned to see the way the older monkeys pushed it away from the food dishes. Being so young, it would probably fare better in a smaller cage on its own. It would be best to have someone to help when I caught it, but the boys weren't due back until five o'clock the next morning and I would have to leave three hours after that on the first lap of my journey back to England. Better to catch the monkey now, I thought.

At that moment the baby obliged by jumping on to the wire beside the door. I opened it quietly, but as soon as I took hold of the monkey by the tail and neck it started screaming. In the second or two it took me to detach its clinging hands from the wire, Kitty became enraged. It wasn't her baby, but as leader of the group she felt responsible for the welfare of all of them. She leapt up on a shelf at the far side of the pen and screamed her anger at me. She bounced up and down on her front feet, crying: 'Hooo, hooo, hoooooo.' I speeded up the operation, knowing that an attack by an adult capuchin can be more lethal than that of an Alsatian.

As I backed out of the door carrying the baby capuchin, Kitty leapt at me from the head-high shelf. As she hurtled through the air towards me, I dropped the baby and ducked swiftly, letting Kitty's impetus carry her over my back and into the compound. As soon as she touched the ground, she turned to attack again, screaming her anger all the time. The baby scrambled up a nearby tree and the other adult capuchin bolted out of the open door just behind me. As I spun round to face Kitty I slammed the door shut with my foot to keep the other two monkeys in.

Kitty was coming at me fast, her eyes full of fury and her bared teeth warning me of my immediate fate. With no defensive weapon within reach, there was only one thing I could do. I bent low, spread my arms wide and yelling at the top of my voice I charged to meet her. Luckily for me, her nerve broke and she veered to one side with a squeal of fright.

The baby set off through the tree-tops away from camp, and after a moment's hesitation the other two capuchins followed. I watched them go, knowing there was nothing I could do. We would never be able to catch those animals in that wilderness.

I was working desultorily around camp about an hour later when the branches of the tree beside the capuchin-pen began to shake and I saw Kitty and the other adult peering down at the two monkeys still in the pen. They jumped down on top of the cage, completely unabashed and showing neither aggression nor shyness of me. They kept just out of my reach, however, and without someone to help me guard the door I couldn't get them back into the pen without the other two escaping. Kitty shook the door and tried to open it, then sat and stared at me reproachfully. They were still hungry, after an unusually meagre breakfast, and although there were plenty of wild berries growing on the island they knew a better place where they could get bananas and mangoes and cucumbers.

I sat down thoughtfully and watched them, leaping and swinging in the trees, plucking leaves, nibbling them and throwing them away, shinning down to the ground, darting into the supply tents and out again, across the monkey-pen and back up into the trees, never moving out of sight of camp. They looked wonderful. This, I thought, was how the animals should be seen, free but showing no shyness or fear of people. But the wild animals of the South American forest would never be seen like this, with the occasional exception of the Howler Monkeys; for the jungle was too vast and thick, and the animals too timid of man, for the keenest observer to be able to see more than the rarest brief glimpse of them.

111

When the baby coatis escaped that day, I hadn't been too surprised at their return to us, excepting for their ability to actually find their way back through the forest. They were, after all, tame and young and had no memory of being free in the wild. But the two monkeys were different. They had been caught as adults only four weeks ago, a few days before I bought them. They weren't tame and never would be, and memories of freedom must still be fresh in their minds. Yet they had come back.

A small thought, tentative and unbelieving, trickled into my mind. Would it be possible, I wondered, to make an island wildlife sanctuary of tame and semi-tame animals and birds, where they all lived free and uncaged? Where food would be set out each day for them, and the forest having been thinned a little and the animals having shed their shyness, people for the first time ever would be able to come and watch New World animals by their hundreds in their natural habitat?

At first I shrugged off the idea. There would be countless difficulties attached to such a project and if it had really been feasible someone would already have done it. But I kept remembering, like a persistent refrain, that Kitty came back.

There was no sign of the baby capuchin and I searched the forest without success. Unfortunately we never found any trace of it and I think it must have fallen prey to a predator in that first hour of freedom. But even in that sad moment of dying, it had already inadvertently caused the first birth-pang of my great idea.

Joe, Naz, Vernon and Milda arrived at noon with my supplies. They helped me get the two capuchins back into the pen, which was a simple job now that I had plenty of bananas to tempt them, had lunch with me, spent a while helping me to search for the baby monkey, and then set off back to Wineperu in the afternoon.

My solitude, totally welcome now that I had plenty of food for the animals, wasn't to last long. I was lying on my bed reading at about ten o'clock that evening when I heard the faint sound of a drum from the other side of the island. Knowing full well there were no Amerindian tribes within a hundred miles, I realised at once that Joe and the others were staging an 'Indian invasion', paddling quietly downstream to my

112

island and anchoring in a dark inlet while they beat the drum that usually hung on Joe's wall.

Putting on my knife-belt—in case I met anything more dangerous than grown men playing cowboys and Indians in the jungle—I slipped out of the tent and into the surrounding forest. The next half-hour was spent by both groups creeping around the island in darkness and trying their hardest to ambush each other.

It ended when I circled back towards camp, creeping silently along the river bank. The moon suddenly sailed out from behind some clouds and revealed a ludicrous situation. The boat was gliding along beside me, a few feet away, with the four of them bent hushed over their paddles, which rose and dipped silently. For forty yards we had stealthily stalked each other on a parallel course, separated by not more than eight feet. In the shout of laughter that followed, they paddled up to our jetty and carried a crate of coke out of the boat. It was the Fearsome Four again, Joe, Naz, Milda and Vernon.

'We thought you might be lonely,' Joe said, and ignored my denials.

In the end they stayed the night. There were plenty of camp beds, but only three of them were assembled.

'Naz and Milda can have Peter's and Keith's beds,' I said, 'but you two men will have to assemble your own beds.'

I frowned warningly as Vernon began to grin. Joe, as yet, didn't know what diabolical contraptions these beds were to assemble and I thought it would be interesting to see him discover the fact. Vernon had frequently stayed overnight on the island and we had already taught him the finer points of fitting the tubes and canvas together. The legs were the worst part, each pair being a thin, shaped metal rod, the two ends of which had to be braced firmly into holes in the bed's tubular frame. There was a certain indefinable knack to this, a necessary last heave that resulted in a faint click as the legs locked into position. Without that locking, things were liable to happen.

'Let's get cracking, Vernon,' Joe said amiably. 'We'll soon get these things put together.'

Vernon assembled his bed swiftly and competently, while Joe watched and copied him. Vernon finished first and lay back on his bed with his hands behind his head as he watched Joe, who had reached the stage of bracing the legs into his own bed. We all watched expectantly as he progressed with cheerful ineptitude.

Heaving and grunting, he managed to get both pairs of legs into position. Still kneeling on the floor, he slapped his hands on his thighs and beamed around at us. He ducked just in time as one pair of legs catapulted over his head and landed with a clatter on the other side of the tent.

'Dear me,' he said mildly, 'perhaps I didn't get it quite right.'

We stifled our laughs as he retrieved the metal legs and fitted them on again, his face a picture of concentration. Slowly he bent the rod and forced the ends into the tubular frame. He let go slowly, cautiously; it stayed in position. But I hadn't heard the faint click to indicate that it had locked.

Holding his hands out like a magician, Joe carefully rose to his feet and inched backwards.

'Don't breathe, anyone,' he said softly. 'I think it's going to work this time.'

Perhaps it was the vibration of his voice that did it, for simultaneously the legs flew off the bed and sailed right through the door of the tent.

Our laughter was unrestrained now as Joe went out to fetch the rod. The patience on his face was slightly strained as he came back, and he gave a hard stare at the bed that Vernon had just assembled, which despite his wild rolls of mirth was showing no signs of collapse.

Joe's next attempt was more successful. The legs stayed put, even when he turned the bed up the right way and tested it cautiously with his hand. He lowered himself on to it very gingerly and slowly lay back. He began to relax as he realised at last that he had beaten the monster. He put his hands behind his head and grinned round at us.

'It's a simple case of intelligence and commonsense,' he began.

With a metallic screech of protest, the legs folded over and the bed crashed to the floor. Above the sound of our hysterical laughter, I could hear Joe roaring: 'Naz, as your employer I demand to have your bed!'

11

A Run of Trouble

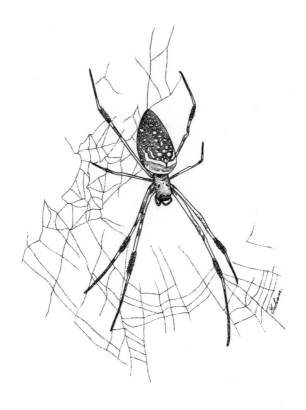

SPIDER

So far our stay at Wineperu had been comparatively peaceful. But when I returned ten days later with the five tourists, Ann, Michael, Pete, Derek and Arthur, everything started happening at once. For several days, in a world that suddenly seemed to have gone berserk, I raced around putting wrongs back to right, sorting out difficulties and reorganising things. There were times when I longed to be alone somewhere in the jungle with no worries, no work, no responsibilities and no people.

I had three main difficulties; no cook, troublesome outboard motors, and a collection of animals that were out of condition after my absence.

There just wasn't time for me to do everything myself and I frequently faced the problem of choosing where my first duty lay. I had a responsibility towards the tourists, which entailed cooking for ten people three times a day, getting the outboards serviced at a time when the machine workshop in Wineperu was on strike, keeping the daily schedule of trips running and sorting out the tourists' minor disagreements. At the same time I was responsible for the welfare of the animals, and I could not ignore their obvious needs. On most days I had to pack in about nineteen or twenty hours' work.

The problems with Joe's outboard motors were serious. We relied on them completely for obtaining supplies from the bush shop in Wineperu and for taking the tourists out each day to the creeks, rapids, islands and beaches where they could swim and fish, and to the mainland for walks in the forest. Joe was fully occupied with timber-felling in the deep forest at that time, and was seldom in the village to chase up the mechanics to get the outboards repaired. By the third day after our return only the tiny two-horsepower engine was still working, and this could power only the small twelve-foot boat with a maximum passenger load of three plus boatman. It was little use for our purpose.

'Come on, Vernon,' I said after cooking breakfast for everyone. 'We'll go up to Wineperu and I'll stand over the mechanics with a machete until one of the big outboards is fixed.'

We set off on the three-mile journey in the flimsy-looking craft, the small engine chugging gamely against the tide and current. Before we had gone far it began to rain. We hunched our shoulders and tried to ignore it. The drizzle increased to a downpour, accompanied by great flashes of lightning which lit up the dark lead-coloured sky. We still carried on, for we had seen many such storms before. We had no suspicions that Guyana was about to throw one of her infrequent climatic tantrums.

We were halfway to Wineperu and within sight of its jetty when we heard the wind coming, a moaning wail in the distance that increased in volume with every second that passed. Vernon and I looked at each other, I puzzled and Vernon with dawning realisation. We were about to see something the locals called a 'little hurricane', a short storm of unbelievable violence. I had never seen one before; Vernon had seen a couple, but never from the vantage point of a small boat with a weak engine on a large river.

'Get ready to bail!' he shouted.

There was only a small tin can rolling about in the bottom of the boat. I leaned forward and grabbed it. Then the wind hit us and all hell was let loose. The boat lurched sideways under the onslaught. The heavy rain was driven almost horizontally with the wind and hit us with the painful force of ice particles. The rain and the boiling river blotted out our sight of Wineperu one-and-a-half miles away and Milda, who was standing on the jetty, saw us disappear into a grey turmoil. For twenty minutes she waited and watched, wondering whether we could possibly survive.

The grey haze that hid us from the jetty had reduced our world. All we could see were mountainous waves and faintly, a quarter-mile away to starboard, the forested shore. Our way there was barred by rocks. The tossing boat rapidly collected water and I bailed at top speed with the can, holding on to the side of the bucking boat with my spare hand so that I couldn't be thrown overboard.

I glanced back at Vernon. He was half-crouched over the tiller, his face a mask of concentration as he watched the huge rollers that were building up and tried to steer the boat to meet them head-on. He kept on course up-river. If he once tried to turn away from the waves they would swamp us. At least we were clear of the rocks if we stayed on this course.

The sheet of rain hitting us in a constant lashing stream was icily cold. Both of us were pinched-looking and blue, shivering uncontrollably. Occasionally, despite all Vernon's efforts, a wave would hit us amidships and the tepid river water that poured over us seemed like a warm bath to our numbed bodies.

As the half-filled boat wallowed I bailed frantically to get the water level down before the next giant wave bore down on us. Each time a wave broke over us before we could rise to its crest, the outboard engine coughed and spluttered and almost died, while Vernon desperately coaxed its feeble spark. Without the small power of the engine we would capsize within a few seconds. The noise was deafening: the high-pitched scream of the wind, the ear-splitting booms of thunder, the pounding of the waves, the sound of a million trees on shore fighting the wind and the tearing crash of a few of them losing that fight and toppling to the forest floor two hundred feet below.

We had been battling the storm for ten minutes when I turned and looked a question at Vernon. It was impossible to use our voices, for the wind snatched the words from our lips and tore them to shreds. For a moment he just looked back at me without his set expression altering, while the boat was thrown about like a piece of driftwood. He knew what I was asking. How long could the boat be pounded like this without breaking up? How long would our stiff and frozen bodies be able to go on working? How much longer could we survive?

The scene around us was fantastic: the Atlantic-like rollers, the solid sheet of rain, lightning splitting the black sky, the forest on shore bent almost double in the massive wind. The elements were throwing everything they had at us in a spectacular show of nature's power. But although we were so small in comparison, they still hadn't beaten us. And if we had to die, we both thought at that moment, then what more magnificent and flamboyant way to die than this? As Vernon looked at me our telepathic thoughts made us both smile at the same instant. Suddenly we were revelling in our fight with the storm. In our sheer joy of the battle the sound of our laughter

118

could be heard above the wild wind. It was the most compelling sensation I have ever experienced.

Ten minutes later Milda saw the grey haze disperse as the wind died away as suddenly as it had begun. The river sank back upon itself, the water level considerably higher now, and the rain settled to a steady downpour. To her relief she saw our boat in almost the same position as its last sighting twenty minutes before. The engine had held us and given us a measure of manoeuvrability, but hadn't allowed us to gain ground.

But now, as the waves subsided, we began to move forward again. When at last we climbed stiffly on to the jetty, shivering violently, Milda was there to meet us, her long black hair plastered wetly to her face. The rain had stopped for a moment, but the lightning and thunder increased until the ground seemed to shake. We reached a wooden shack just as a few large spots of rain began to fall again and we took shelter on the verandah in time to avoid another cloudburst.

We were only there a few seconds when a particularly violent flash of lightning split the sky and as we were deafened by the crack of thunder a metal electricity pole a few feet from us crackled and leaned sideways amid leaping sparks as lightning struck it. We all jumped nervously and stared at the blackened pole, counting the few feet separating us.

'Oh, please,' I said weakly, 'we've had enough excitement for one day!'

It was four hours before Vernon and I stopped shaking with cold and by then our jaws were aching from the effects of our teeth chattering involuntarily. But the journey had been worthwhile, as I managed to get one of the big outboards repaired. The mechanics may have been tough men striking for a good cause, but they hadn't the heart to turn this wretched waif away empty-handed. A woollen blanket, bought from the bush-shop, was wrapped around me over my wet clothes, my face was mottled white and blue, and a combination of stiff lips and chattering teeth made it almost impossible to talk, although they eventually understood that I wanted the 'b-b-bloody outb-b-board fixed'. Vernon and I found ourselves treated rather as heroes in the village for surviving the little hurricane in a small boat, and the owner of the bush-shop

119

gave us mugs of scalding tea laced with rum with his compliments.

On the fourth day after our arrival at Murray Island there was the only serious accident of our whole stay in South America. Luckily it happened to me, and not to any of the tourists in my care. It had been a very rushed day—every day was, at that time—as the outboards were still giving us a lot of trouble.

Everyone had just returned from spending a day on the river with Vernon and before starting to cook supper for the ten of us I made them a pot of tea. Hurrying into the tent with it I stepped on an unsuspected patch of kerosene that someone had spilt on the groundsheet. I had no sensation of falling. One moment I was on my feet, and the next the world had exploded in pain as I landed on my back with such force that I was almost stunned.

The first few moments as I lay there were rather frightening, because I could feel the numbness in my legs and couldn't move them. I thought I'd broken my back. In a minor way I had, for the lower part of my spine—the tail-bone—had snapped and been pushed thirty degrees out of alignment. But this seemed nothing in comparison to my first unspoken fears that I was paralysed. After a few moments I found I could move my legs slightly, although it sent stabs of pain through my stomach and along my back. Two of the men lifted me bodily and placed me in a chair. Gentle as they tried to be, I broke out in a sweat at the pain.

I had given a doctor a free trip along with the tourists in case any of them became hurt, and logically Richard was the person I should have consulted at that moment. But I went out of my way to avoid him. As long as I wasn't certain that the base of my spine was broken then I was prepared to carry on. If my suspicion was confirmed then I would only have the added worry that moving about would cause further injury. Looking back now, I'm sure I did the wisest thing in carrying on—apart from the fact that I didn't have much choice. If I had gone to bed for a few days, it would probably have been several weeks before I was able to walk again. The way I stiffened up after a night in bed, even though I stayed active during each day, convinced me of the need for exercise.

120

As soon as I could get on my feet that first evening I went to the supply tent and swallowed a handful of pain-killers. Everyone helped me to cook supper and then I set off to Wineperu with Vernon to fetch the repaired outboards. I found I could move slowly in a straight line, but if I moved either leg even slightly to the side or put my full weight on my left leg I would gasp involuntarily at the spasm.

I had to hide the pain as much as possible from the tourists, otherwise it would have been embarrassing for me and tiresome for them. Vernon alone realised the extent of my injury; he was a real friend during the following days.

He only referred to the accident once, that first evening after supper when I was trying to climb the steep cliff path in Wineperu to Joe's house. I had to pause frequently to rest while Vernon watched me unhappily. Then he said quietly: 'Chris, I think you're hurt bad.'

'Yes,' I said. There was no use pretending to him, for the gradient almost brought me to my knees once or twice. We never mentioned it again.

But during the following days he watched me constantly from the background, ready to give me unobtrusive help. When I was faced with climbing out of boats, walking up a steep slope, or even stepping over a fallen log, I would hang back and let the others go ahead. As soon as they were out of sight I would lean all my weight on Vernon's shoulder and he would half-lift me over the difficult stretch. Once on flat ground I was able to walk normally again at a slow pace.

Maybe it was silly to pretend to the others that I was only bruised and a bit stiff. Normally I appreciate sympathy as much as the next person, but at that particular time I was in charge of everything and I was supposed to be tough. It was no time to hanker after sympathy. Somehow the whole affair tied up in my mind with the legend that the jungle is no place for a woman. I knew the jungle was close to beating me this time, and I had to fight it on my own.

At least at nights I was alone and had the luxury of not pretending, for I had moved my bed into the big tent that housed the small-animal cages, set away from all the other tents. But the nights were the worst time for pain. My camp bed was only nine inches high, and it was a long and agonising job getting down to it and back on to my feet in the mornings. Once asleep, it was impossible to control movement and the slightest shifting of my legs or back provoked a flash of pain that woke me again.

For the first three nights I could do little more than cat-nap, lying rigidly in my narrow bed and talking softly to the baby black coatimundi curled beneath my chin. Every time I fell asleep and an incautious movement tumbled me back into shocked wakefulness again the coati woke up too, squeaking worriedly, pushing his tiny rubbery nose into my face and licking the tears on my cheeks until I settled him under my chin again and stroked him back to sleep.

Although I was unable to sleep properly, at least I could use the time for some uninterrupted thinking, which was always impossible during the daytime. It was the jungle that occupied most of my thoughts. Apart from the vast and sometimes harsh factual landscape, there were so many intangible aspects of the jungle: the excitement, danger, peace, personal fears and, for some, a terrifying sense of loneliness. There was also humour. The jungle has so many weapons, physical and mental, with which to repel our intrusion that man's own weapons—his intelligence, knowledge, machinery and equipment—seem feeble by comparison. But our greatest single weapon has been our sense of humour. With our ability to turn discomfort and disaster into a joke we are able to overcome anything the jungle can produce to deter us. Without humour, we couldn't survive very long out there.

I began to think about the wild animals, for me, at least, the most important aspect of the jungle. Although they had freedom, theirs were no lives of comfort and leisure. There could be no relaxation in their watch for danger, no shelter from the storms and the cold rain that sometimes fell for days on end. Each day or night was an endless search for sufficient food for the fruit-eaters, for the jungle was nothing like the popular concept of wild fruits growing on every tree.

The baby coati sighed and stretched in his sleep and snuggled closer to my neck. I tickled his fat tummy and his mobile nose wiggled in delight while his eyes stayed closed. Would he be happier out in the dark wet forest without us, even if he had his mother's company? I didn't think so.

My thoughts turned again to an island sanctuary. It would not only be a wonderful place for people who were interested in animals; more important, it would give the animals the best of both worlds. They would still have their freedom, but they would no longer have to contend with predators and hunger.

So this is the jungle, I thought. Not just millions of green trees, but people and animals as well, and humour, peace, danger, loneliness and beauty. Not just a place, but a way of life. If I could get through this latest challenge without giving up then I could be positive that this was the life I wanted permanently and that it wouldn't be able to break my spirit.

A couple of days after I hurt my back, three of the tourists, Derek, Pete and Arthur, had a very narrow escape in the rapids and were saved only by Vernon's quick-thinking and instant action. With one of the bigger outboards now repaired Vernon had taken them three miles upstream to see the tumbling rapids, a mile wide and nearly as long. The river-level was rapidly dropping at the end of the rainy season and the water roared and raced white-foamed between newly-exposed rocks.

From long years of experience, Vernon knew where the safest routes through the rapids lay. But with the intense concentration that always made his face set into hard lines when he was pitting his wits against the Essequibo, he watched with care the inconstant currents of the flowing mass of water. Whirlpools had formed in places, and in others a stretch of water would be pulled two ways by the currents, half flowing south and the other half north.

They were driving out of the lee of one of the many small rocky islands when a six-foot wave gathered itself on the far side of the island, rolled down on them and broke over the stern half of the long boat. It missed the three tourists up in the bows, but in the stern Vernon had no chance to see it coming until the great crest hit him with stunning force. He gripped the gunwale to prevent himself being swept away as hundreds of gallons of water poured over him. The big outboard motor caught the full force of the wave. It was lifted from its base, the bolts shearing off, and was swept over the side where it sank in several fathoms of water.

The wave subsided and Vernon, still half-blinded by the

water, summed up the danger of their situation in one swift glance. The slowly spinning boat had been caught by the powerful current. It was already almost past the tiny rocky island, being swept down towards a stretch of boiling white water where the jagged half-submerged rocks showed as a mass of black teeth.

It had all happened in an instant and the other three men looked surprised rather than scared as Vernon ran between them to the bows, picked up the long rope painter and dived overboard. He surfaced several yards away, waist-deep in water on the shores of the island. Bracing himself backwards, he pulled on the rope. The boat came to a halt, the water racing past on either side of it. Inch by inch he strained to pull the boat nearer and as soon as it was out of deep water the tourists tumbled overboard and helped him pull it in and beach it on the hard rock.

Their situation, although temporarily safer, was still precarious. Nobody would worry about their absence until dusk, which meant no search-party over this dangerous stretch of river until dawn the next day. The island was barren rock, with no bushes even as cover, and it was continually drenched with a fine spray from the tumbling water. It would mean severe exposure for the unacclimatised tourists, first from the hot afternoon sun and then from the cold and wet of the eleven-hour night.

The outboard motor had been tied to the boat by a long cord, so the men were able to salvage it. But full of water it was no use until all the parts had been dried out in less damp conditions than the island offered.

Vernon had a paddle in the boat; none of the outboard-motorised boats ever went out without one. For a long time he stood gazing down-river, trying to decide a course of action. He had been through the rapids without a motor before, but never without another experienced boatman in the bows to watch and warn him of rocks just beneath the surface. And he had never paddled through the rapids when the water-level had temporarily dropped to this dangerous half-way stage where the flow was particularly fast and hundreds of rocks were newly-exposed.

At last Vernon made up his mind. He seated two of the

124

tourists amidships and the third one up in the bows, telling him to point out any underwater rocks in their path, but knowing that his inexperienced eyes wouldn't see them until the moment of impact. The three visitors were a little apprehensive, but as Vernon was so calm they saw no cause to be afraid. No face is so passive and unexpressive as that of a worried Amerindian.

And so they came pell-mell down the rapids, caught by the rushing water, twisting and turning as Vernon steered them through the cataract, grating harshly over a few hidden rocks, but emerging breathless and triumphant on the other side. After the long, slow journey down the next part of the river, they arrived in camp at dusk.

Pete, Derek and Arthur were excited about their adventure, scarcely realising the appalling danger they had been in. Without Vernon's split-second decision to dive overboard they would have been swept past the island and on to the rocks, where the boat would have been pounded to pieces. I praised Vernon's skill and courage, but added darkly: 'You'd have had some explaining to do to me if you'd lost any of my tourists!'

He grinned. 'I'd already thought of that,' he admitted.

Funnily enough, the next evening's incident scared the tourists far more, although it was a farce that even Brian Rix in his wilder moments could never have created.

Just after supper somebody suggested we went creek-drifting and everyone else supported the idea enthusiastically. Creek-drifting in Guyana is a delightful occupation. The watery byways slide quietly into the forest, narrow and winding. The impressive power of the Essequibo is left behind and the clear russet-brown water moves softly. Late afternoon is the best time to go, when the sun slants through the trees in little pools of amber and a lazy somnolence lies over the forest. We motor a mile or two up a creek until there is insufficient draught to go further, then we silence the engine and wait for peace to settle after the disturbance of our passing.

Then we let the slow current take the boat, drifting lazily downstream through a tunnel of trees. Using the paddles only to guide the boat around bends and the occasional moss-covered rock, we dip them carefully so that they make no

125

sound; then we lay them dripping across our knees and relax. Tiny birds dart among the branches, scarcely noticing our noiseless passing, and unseen greenheart birds call with a pure echoing voice from the tops of the tallest trees. A purple-and-black morpho butterfly floats ahead of us, low over the water and then off through the trees on large velvety wings. We glide past a flowering bush where a hundred butterflies drift in a coloured cloud.

The air is rich with the smell of leaf-mould and moss and damp wood, and long rays of sunshine trickle across the dark water in little rivulets. The song of a bird and the ripple of water sliding round a rock only serve to emphasise the great silence and the tangible atmosphere of deep peace.

Another good time to go creek-drifting is at night. Although it is eerie, there is always a chance of seeing some of the forest animals come down to drink. A small boat and only three or four people are the best conditions, but that evening Vernon and I found ourselves with the largest boat and six people clamouring to come.

I took up a paddle in the bows, with Vernon in the stern as usual. Seated between us in the long, narrow boat were Michael, Ann, Derek, Pete, Arthur and Richard, the doctor. We motored two miles upstream from the island and spent an hour drifting about the gloomy creek, our torches extinguished as we wandered with the current. It was a creepy setting for anyone nervous about the unseen dangers of the jungle. Barely-seen rocks and trees loomed slowly as black shadows in a black night and glided past us. A wet cluster of leaves brushed gently over a bare arm and a fragile cobweb caught a face, sticky and clinging.

We were not lucky enough to see any animals that night, and back in the main river I suggested to Vernon that we paddle down to a small island where we had frequently seen some capybara that went there each night to graze. We set off down-river in darkness. When we reached the tiny island we dipped our paddles very carefully so that they made no noise. We slid silently down one side of the island, rounded the tip and began to paddle up the other side against the current, twenty feet out from the shore.

The silence was suddenly broken by the sound of some

126

creature racing across the water from the island. It hit the side of the boat and landed amongst the tourists with a heavy thump. There was instant pandemonium. The boat rocked and bucked as they threw themselves with one accord away from the unseen intruder. The people who had torches in their hands ready to turn on dropped them in the stampede, and Vernon's and mine, placed close to our sides while we paddled, were kicked away by thrashing feet.

The creature, whatever it was, ran or jumped noisily from one end of the boat to the other and there were shouts and screams as its wet slimy body touched bare legs and the faces of one or two unlucky people who had been knocked down in the rush. At either end of the boat, Vernon and I were on our hands and knees groping for a torch, getting our fingers trampled on in the process. To say that we were concerned about the panic amongst our passengers is an understatement. At any moment we expected the boat to capsize; eight of us struggling in the river in total darkness would be no joke.

'Everyone sit down and stay still,' I bellowed, feeling like a lone soldier trying to quell a Zulu war. Nobody took any notice. I can't say I blamed them, for the new arrival could be anything from a giant anaconda to a piranha or a jungle-cat. At that moment my bruised fingers touched a rolling torch. I turned on the switch and the beam lit up a fantastic scene.

Two of the tourists were crouched on the gunwale ready to abandon ship. Beyond the centre cross-seat was a tangled pile of bodies with arms and legs sticking out at impossible angles. Heads swivelled as the beam of my torch swept the scuppers searching for the uninvited guest amongst us. The light fastened on a foot-long perfectly harmless lukanani fish that was flapping about helplessly.

Vernon broke the short silence that followed.

'Fish for breakfast, mistress,' he announced solemnly.

'My God!' Derek rejoined feelingly, nursing a black-eye received from a flaying elbow. 'There *must* be an easier way of catching them!'

12

The Kaieteur Trail

Dennis, Valerie and Brian should have arrived on Murray Island with their animals almost simultaneously with me arriving with the tourists. But they didn't come. Peter and Keith thought of all manner of reasons for the delay, but by the time I was due to leave again eight days later it was obvious even to them that the others would never come now. Their faces were stony with disappointment and they began to talk of abandoning the island.

I was irretrievably committed to completing the rest of the tour and I felt desperate concern for the fate of the animals on the island. At last I managed to get Keith and Peter to promise that they would stay there and look after them for another ten days, giving me time to finish the tour and see the tourists off from Georgetown on their flight. Then I would come straight back to Murray Island to take over, and Keith and Peter would be free to go as they wanted. I felt a tight knot of anxiety for the animals as I left with the tourists, but there was nothing I could do except put my trust in the two men.

Ann, Michael, Derek, Pete, Arthur and Richard travelled with me to Bartica and from there we went by air to Kangaruma where we stayed the night. The following morning we made the six-hour journey up the Potaro River to Tukeit Rest House, no more than a collection of ramshackle wooden huts, but with a certain primitive charm all of its own. From there we would be able to trek to the Kaieteur Falls. The managers, Mr and Mrs Bell, were there to greet us.

Mrs Bell reminded me of an overblown floribunda rose. A Guyanese of African descent, she had a gentle personality and short wiry hair dressed in a multitude of small stiff plaits that stood out from her head like a prickly halo. She was wailing loudly when we arrived and a large white cloth was tied around her plump face. Mrs Bell had toothache.

'Mistress, I sick in de toot,' she howled by way of introduction, holding the side of her face and swaying like a mountain in an earthquake. 'I no sleep for t'ree days, de pain so bahd! I no eat food for t'ree days, mistress, soon I t'ink I starve!' Her vast bosom quivered as she wailed again.

'I've got a doctor here who'll put you right in no time at all,' I reassured her.

Richard was trailing up the slope from the river, weighted down with a rucksack and a box of food.

'Your first patient in Guyana,' I greeted him. 'Mrs Bell has toothache. I've told her you'll cure her with your special medicine.'

Richard looked doubtful.

'Otherwise,' I said with careful emphasis, '*we* shall have to do the cooking tonight.'

'I'll do my best,' he said in faint alarm.

He ushered Mrs Bell into her hut for an examination of the offending molar and packed the cavity with something from his medical bag. When they reappeared fifteen minutes later, Mrs Bell's face was split by a wide melon grin and the cloth was no longer tied around her jaw.

'De Doc he done fix me,' she announced blithely. 'I no get pain now, atall, atall. Mistress, dis mahn he *fine* doctor! You want I cook de food for you tonight?'

Thankfully leaving her sorting over our stores, the rest of us struck out on the trail to the top of the Kaieteur Falls with Mr Bell as our guide. He was a small, quiet man from St Lucia who always wore dark glasses to protect his weak eyes. Whenever he was out he always carried an old rifle tucked under his arm, and knowing how short-sighted he was we found ourselves instinctively ducking whenever he turned our way.

We had to trek at a smart pace as it was getting late and we had to be down off the trail again before dark. The path started off gently enough, meandering through some pleasant open woodland. But soon after crossing a creek the trail began to rise steeply on its long journey to the unseen falls a thousand feet above the level of Tukeit. The trees closed in thickly and the air became moist and warm. The trail became no more than a broken and narrow path of boulders and small loose rocks, all of them covered in wet moss. It was so steep in places that we had to use our hands to help us scramble, while our feet slipped and slithered on the treacherous surface.

The Kaieteur trail is always the subject of animated discussion amongst those who have climbed it. The Visitors' Book at Tukeit is full of pungent comments. The shortest and most explicit is: 'Phew!'

130

Our first climb seemed the worst, especially as several people had told us that the trail was 'not so bad'. It was a while before I learned to appreciate that a trail described by local Guyanese as 'not so bad' meant that it was terrible, and those described as 'not good' were quite impassable.

I like to take at least two hours to climb the Kaieteur trail, pausing many times to regain my breath and admire the scenery. That first afternoon, with Mr Bell urging us along, we were forced to cover it in eighty minutes. Gasping for breath and with the perspiration streaming off us in the humid atmosphere, we climbed after him in a daze.

Soon after I stopped to pick up a dead "two-headed" snake which I found beside the path, the trail became so bad that Ann and Michael decided to turn back. Richard heaved a professional sigh of relief as we watched them go, for Michael weighed all of fifteen stone and we doubted if his heart would stand the strain of the climb. Also being practical, if somewhat heartless, we had wondered how we would ever carry him down the steep broken trail if he collapsed. We were all bedraggled and exhausted wrecks when an hour later the path levelled out and Mr Bell announced, 'Not so far now, mistress, jus' one more li'l hill.'

He disappeared round a bend in the path and we staggered after him, thankful that we had made it. We found him waiting for us where the trail struck off sharply at right angles. It mounted the side of a huge cliff that towered above us like a New York skyscraper.

'Oh, God!' we all said together, our voices desperate.

'Dat what dey call dis part of de trail,' Mr Bell agreed seriously, 'de "Oh-God-Stretch".'

He regarded our flushed and dripping faces and added sympathetically, 'It's not so bad.'

Against our predictions, we managed to climb the last steep stretch and then it was just a long, gentle walk through semi-open country dotted with palms and boulders and strange-looking giant succulents. I felt like crawling the last lap, especially as it was only six days since I had injured my back.

For the past half-hour the others, who had never seen Kaieteur, had often said to me, 'Are you *sure* it's worth it?'

131

Out of breath, I could only nod. They went ahead with Mr Bell on the last stretch and I wandered slowly along behind, gradually recovering my composure. I entered a fairyland of grottoes and flowers and huge scattered rocks, passed through a wet moss-hung tunnel beneath the rocks and emerged on the cliff-face above the gorge opposite the spectacle of the great plunging waterfall. The others' faces were filled with delighted wonder; there was no need to ask whether they thought the climb worthwhile.

The climb itself, being so rugged and strenuous, had been a good build-up to the magnificent finale. It was by this route that explorers first discovered Kaieteur hidden deep in the heart of the jungle. All of us who climbed the trail developed a mild contempt for the tourists who sometimes chose the easy way, flying in to the air-strip and taking an hour's gentle stroll without grazing their shins or straining their lungs, but without experiencing our own sense of achievement by climbing the trail.

We moved around to the head of the falls where we could see the deep, rapid-strewn gorge away in the distance. Wisps of mist floated across the river and a rainbow lay across the rim of the falls where the sun glinted on the spray. A long line of swifts came speeding along the upper course of the river. They swept over the edge of the falls close to the solid sheet of plunging water and three hundred feet down executed a graceful loop and flew through a small gap in the cataract of water to their nesting-grounds in an unseen cave behind the falls. How many hundred years ago, I wondered, did the first bird discover the hidden cave, handing on its knowledge through countless generations of fledglings?

Our descent of the trail was a race with darkness. But even so, we paused a few moments when we saw a very rare sight, a cock-of-the-rock, shyest of all the South American birds, sitting on a branch not thirty yards from us while a flock of parrots tried to mob it. Its flaming orange plumage was like a small glowing fire in the twilight and the square crest on its head was distinct as it ignored its tormentors with calm dignity. It was pure magic for anyone interested in wildlife, one of my greatest moments in Guyana.

We left late next morning, after Derek, Pete, Arthur and

Richard had made another marathon climb to the top of Kaieteur. We stayed the night again at Kangaruma and early the next morning flew south in a rattling, bone-shaking and oven-hot Dakota, to Lethem in the southern savannahs.

We entered an entirely different world from the jungles of the north, a Wild West country where horse-riders ambled down the dusty main street of the biggest town. The savannahs were vast and yellow, coarse grass growing in tangled clumps on poor sandy soil, sparse bushes and giant termite hills, lush palm-lined creeks and scattered Indian villages. The savannah rolled away in all directions until it met the low jungle-clad mountains.

The people were very different from the northerners. There were few Negroes to be seen, most of them being Amerindian, white, or a mixture of both. They were tough, strong-willed people, fiercely independent and proud. They ran their cattle ranches in a big and harsh country, and their personalities were big and determined to match. I loved the savannahs, despite the sweltering heat and the occasional swarms of dreaded kaboura flies. When I drove a bucking mini-moke over the deserted trails, or rode a vaquero pony through the creeks and over the rough land, I was filled with a great sense of freedom. There was so much space, all of it wild and rugged and inspiring.

We camped at Minari Ranch House, pitching the tents down by the creek where the palm-trees rustled in the breeze. Facing east, each dawn was a joy to watch from the comfort of my camp bed, the sweeping fronds of the palms silhouetted against the red and gold glow of the rising sun, while flocks of parakeets screamed and the ranch ponies grazed quietly outside the tent.

We took our meals up at the ranch house, and what fantastic and old-fashioned meals they were! Lunch and dinner differed little, and one was expected to have generous portions of everything: soup, three kinds of meat, four or five different vegetables, bowls of mixed salads, a cooked sweet and fresh fruit. In the extreme heat, our spirit sometimes quailed at the sight of the heavily-laden table, and it was normal for us to leave the table three or four times during a meal to go outside and cool off in the gentle breeze.

133

The tourists hired mini-mokes to explore the surrounding areas and for a few days I found I had nothing to do. As suddenly, I realised how desperately tired I had become and how badly in need of sleep. I fell asleep at odd moments and in odd places, and people frequently came across my slumbering body in a chair on the patio, propped against a shady bank and even curled beside the creek with a fishing-rod clutched in my hand.

My arms and ankles were badly bitten by kaboura flies, minute harmless-looking midges. Swollen and itching madly, I was subdued by the knowledge that each bite would leave a permanent faint bluish scar. The owner of Minari, old Mrs Orella, herself part-Amerindian and a descendant of one of the original British pioneers who brought their cattle and possessions hundreds of miles up-river on rafts, insisted on treating me like an invalid. Each night after dinner she would appear with a bottle of calamine, and taking my feet one by one into her lap she gently smoothed the lotion on to my inflamed legs. She ignored my half-hearted protests, and I secretly enjoyed the sensation of being mothered by this tough but gentle old lady of the savannahs.

Sadly, the area was torn by rebellion between the Government and the ranchers over a land dispute four months later, and many of the friends I made on my two visits were forced to seek refuge over the border. Their ranches lie damaged and neglected, but not forgotten by their absent owners.

As our first stay at Minari drew to a close, events began to wake up again, as if Guyana had decided that I'd had a sufficiency of rest. Michael and Ann started it, on our last full day, by telling an Indian family in one of the villages that I wanted to buy animals. With the situation as it was with the team, the last thing I wanted was more animals until I had re-organised things. But next morning, a few hours before our Dakota was due to leave for Georgetown, I took one of Minari's mini-mokes and set out to find the village, not wanting to let the Indians down if they'd actually caught anything for me. Derek, Pete and Richard decided to come along for the ride, not realising what they were letting themselves in for.

After endless trouble and mis-directions we managed to

find the right village, the right hut and the right Indian girl, Anna. By then I was already glancing at my watch, for we were expected for lunch at Minari before leaving for the airport. Luckily we had dismantled the tents and packed all the equipment earlier. I asked Anna whether she had any animals for me, mentally crossing my fingers and hoping she'd say No.

Her face lit up with a shy smile. 'Oh, yes, we caught animals!'

I tried my best to look pleased. 'What kind of animals?'

'An armadillo.'

Well, that wasn't too bad. Armadillos weren't much trouble to have around.

'And an ant-bear,' she added, looking modest.

My heart fell into my tattered plimsolls. A giant-anteater!

'A *little* ant-bear?' I asked hopefully.

She shook her head so vigorously that her long black plait danced. 'No, a *big* one!' She spread her arms wide to show me.

My mind boggled at the thought of getting a fully-grown and highly-dangerous giant-anteater back to Georgetown without any prior organisation. But as Anna and her husband had worked so hard and risked their lives catching it for us, I could hardly confess that I didn't really want it.

Anna's husband was with the captured animal at a friend's hut two miles away. Anna pointed at a foot-track that led away behind their own hut. A mini-moke is only built to carry four people, but we sat Anna on Pete's lap, and Anna's small baby on *her* lap, Derek took the wheel and we set off.

We travelled in bottom gear, the engine screaming as we reared up over banks, ploughed through mud-holes and cautiously drove through two shallow creeks. As we went, Anna told us how she and her husband lay in wait for the anteater the night before, lassoed it with a cowhide rope and tied it to a tree. Then they built a stockade around it and managed to lash its feet together.

I was full of admiration for their feat. Although a giant-anteater is toothless, its front feet are equipped with massive claws for tearing open cement-hard termite hills so that its long whip-like sticky tongue can gather the insects. The claws are so thick and long that the animal is forced to walk on its knuckles with the claws folded back. When cornered, the normally peaceful anteater will face its enemy and rear up, over five feet tall. One sweep of its forepaw can disembowel a man.

I reached the friend's hut and found the two Indian men standing guard over the trussed anteater. I was worried about the tourists' lunch, for they were supposed to be enjoying a holiday, but they voted enthusiastically to help me with the animal and never mind about missing lunch; they'd already eaten too much at Minari, anyway.

I paid Anna's husband for the anteater and armadillo, and for another four Guyanese dollars I bought his friend's dining-room table. This was a big, stout wooden box, and with some thick planks to nail over the open top it made a good crate for the ant-bear.

The anteater was truculent but helpless as we lifted it and lowered it into the crate. I didn't like doing it, but I had to leave its legs trussed together during the journey. It was not only the danger to the tourists in leaving those lethal paws free even momentarily while we nailed down the lid, but also the fact that the crate would be travelling in the same cabin in the 'plane as ourselves and other passengers. My heart quailed at the thought of an untied giant-anteater breaking out of a crate in a confined cabin when we were two thousand feet above a vast tract of jungle mountains. I didn't think the pilot would like it.

I was constantly glancing at my watch. We'd not only missed lunch, but if we didn't hurry we would miss our 'plane. We collapsed the canvas roof of the mini-moke and managed to wedge the five-foot-long crate across the top of the rear seat, one end of it jutting over the passenger's front seat.

Fitting us all in wasn't easy. Richard sat on the floor at the back, a space little more than a foot wide, together with the armadillo in a sack. I perched on top of the folded hood, steadying the crate beside me. Peter took the front passenger seat again, in imminent danger of being decapitated if the crate slipped, Anna and the baby sat on his lap. Anna's husband clung to the outside of the vehicle, Derek got behind the wheel and we took off—or groaned off would be more accurate. The tiny vehicle could hardly be seen for its load.

In a mad-cap chase across the savannahs, we dropped Anna and her husband off at their hut, and got to the airport with only minutes to spare. Having got the anteater on to the 'plane, I then spent the flight pondering the problem of where to house it when we reached Georgetown. The manager of the Belvedere Hotel, Mr Deally, had let me keep animals in my room there on several occasions, even after one of his maids fled shrieking along the corridor, down the stairs and into the street with a baby coatimundi gambolling playfully at her heels. Mr Deally took my side.

'Stupid woman,' he commented, referring to the maid, 'she should never have gone into your room while you were out—she ought to know what to expect in there by now!'

Snakes, parrots, monkeys, alligators, tree-porcupines, Mr Deally's amiable smile never slipped. But a fully-grown giant-anteater was a bit different.

When we reached the Belvedere, four lucky people disappeared upstairs for a cool bath, an air-conditioned rest, to be followed by a leisurely meal. Derek and Pete, bless their eager hearts, stuck with me, determined to see this thing through to the end. We left the crate in the minibus I'd hired and wandered round to the back of the hotel seeking anteater accommodation. We were peering into some concrete bunkers when Mr Deally came trotting by and beamed at us. I called him over.

'I was wondering,' I said casually, 'whether I could keep a rather large giant-anteater in here for a few days?'

He gave a hard look at the bunker we were inspecting and tut-tutted. 'If it's too small,' he said helpfully, 'there's a bigger one at the end.'

He was surprised when we laughed, and even more surprised when I exclaimed: 'Mr Deally, you're wonderful!'

But before I inflicted a giant-anteater on the Belvedere guests, I decided to investigate another more suitable solution that occurred to me. The minibus took us out to Kitty, a suburb of Georgetown, to the yard of an animal-dealer, Mr Low, who had supplied me with a number of animals and was trying to get some particular species for us. He proved to be very co-operative about my problem and changed some of his animals around to leave the biggest cage free for the giant-anteater.

We pried the lid of the crate loose and I wanted to put the animal in the cage before we cut its bonds and put some cream on its chafed ankles, so that if it turned nasty we had only to slam the door on it. But she (for some unknown reason we had already started calling it she, although about the only way to sex a giant-anteater is to put another giant-anteater with it and see what they do) was so docile lying there in her box that Mr Low insisted that it was quite safe to cut her free there and tend the grazes.

Pete, a black-bearded softly-spoken teacher from the north, agreed with me. 'She were in a right mood when we crated her,' he warned Mr Low.

'I can handle her,' Mr Low said confidently. He stroked the animal and spoke quietly for a few moments, and then cut the ropes free. She lay quietly while cream was smoothed on to her sore ankles. But as soon as we began to move the box to the cage-door, she erupted into life. We scattered in all directions to avoid her flailing front feet. I was astonished at the great roar that came out of her tiny mouth, little more than a narrow tube in the long nose. There was only one feeble light bulb in the yard, and it was long since dark; her shadow as she stood reared up and swaying looked monstrous.

Then she dropped to all fours and charged Mr Low, rearing up just before she reached him. He leapt on top of a stack of cages with surprising agility for a heavy-set man. The anteater turned and charged Derek and Pete, who were standing close together.

'Look out!' I yelled, with visions of two coffins on tomorrow's flight for England. The result of my shout and seeing the animal thundering towards them was remarkable. There were only two trees in Mr Low's yard, but they chose one apiece and shot up them like scalded cats, disappearing out of the faint circle of light.

I was so intrigued by their prowess in climbing trees that I was still standing there open-mouthed when the anteater caught sight of me and came running. I snatched up a heavy plank of wood and fended it off. I couldn't climb to safety anywhere, as there were only some low, flimsy cages close to hand. But as the anteater slowly forced me back, I finally took refuge by squeezing myself into the narrow gap between the cages and the wall and thankfully watched her shuffle off.

There was a short silence as we all regained our breath. Then I heard Pete's voice floating down from the top of his tree. 'Mr Low,' he gently admonished, 'ah towd you she were dangerous!'

It was another hour before we managed to get the anteater in the cage; by then it was ten o'clock, and we hadn't eaten or washed since breakfast. Our plans for a farewell supper were ruined, and what was worse one of my animals had put Derek and Pete up a tree. I apologised to them feelingly.

'But I enjoyed it,' Derek exclaimed.

'Eh, lass,' Peter said earnestly, 'it were best part o' tour!'

It was after we caged the anteater that I noticed several of my animals from the island in the yard. Mr Low thought I knew that Keith and Peter had brought him the collection to look after, and such was his amiability that he hadn't thought to mention it when I turned up with the giant-anteater and asked if I could leave it there for a few days.

Peter and Keith had abandoned Murray Island three days after my departure. They had freed some of the animals. The rest they had brought back to Georgetown; the ones that didn't die on the journey were handed over to Mr Low to care for until my return. They'd brought the team tents and equipment back with them, but left my own tents behind in Bartica. It was a bitter moment, but slightly eased when Mr Low said he'd look after them all until I returned to England in five weeks' time. Another good thing was that he'd managed to obtain a true pair of baby tapirs, which I wanted specially.

My final weeks in Guyana, like the preceding ones, were a fairly even mixture of good and bad. But I think the bad parts of trips like these are always more than cancelled out by the good parts. Peter, Keith and I brought the team accounts up to date, and wound up the team affairs. As I had paid for the animals with my own money, it was agreed that they should stay mine.

The second camping tour contained none of the near-disasters and difficulties that made the first tour such hard work. Instead, I had time to really enjoy looking after the visitors, including a highly combustible Frenchwoman, Janine and a fishing-mad Londoner, Harry Halford. By the time we returned to Georgetown we were lasting friends, already impatient for the day when they could come back to the jungle with me, perhaps as first visitors to my tentatively planned island sanctuary.

My collection of animals at Mr Low's yard had grown, and he agreed to dispatch them by air to me two days after my own departure to England. I paid one last visit to Mr Low to arrange the final details. While I was there, I looked into the cages to see if there were any new arrivals.

I dropped to my knees in front of a low cage, for I had caught a glimpse of two curious faces amid shaggy capes of brown fur. I was elated to find I was right. One face was white-furred and the other brown with a yellow streak on each cheek: a pair of white-faced Saki monkeys.

'Mr Low,' I called softly, hardly daring to breathe. 'Are these two sold?'

'Not yet.'

Their price was £10. I paid without bargaining. I knew what I was taking on, how delicate and temperamental they were. But I was determined to will them to live, to use every ounce of effort to overcome the difficulties of acclimatising them in England.

In their way these memorable monkeys did much to keep alive my dream of one day making a wild-life sanctuary on a jungle island, the place I shall call Saki Island Sanctuary.

13

The Old Man and His Missus
Come to Britain

CAPYBARA

I paced up and down the BOAC freight office at Heathrow Airport as nervously as any expectant father in a hospital waiting room. I had arrived back in England only the previous Friday, with just a weekend to prepare my flat in Cobham, Surrey, for the arrival of the animals.

The Georgetown flight had arrived a short while ago, but although one of the officials told me that all the animals seemed to have survived the journey, I still hadn't been allowed to see them. They had been in the crates for twenty hours and although they would have been supplied with plenty of food and water I wondered what kind of condition they were in.

Most of the stock was reasonably hardy for travelling: capuchin and squirrel monkeys, parrots, parakeets, toucans, various species of snakes, coatimundis, a tree-porcupine and a baby armadillo. But there were several more delicate animals that needed a lot of care.

A London Zoo van man waited to take a pair of Tamandua anteaters and the tree-porcupine direct to their prepared quarters in the zoo. And there were a valuable pair of baby tapirs; another van waited to take them straight to their new owner. Tapirs, however young, were one species that even I, with all my optimism, had to admit were beyond the capacity of my first-floor flat.

But the main reason for my nervous pacing was the pair of very delicate monkeys, my Sakis. Sakis are not so rare in the wild as might be imagined, although as they live in pairs and trios instead of in large troupes few actually come into the hands of exporters. But the fact that none of the zoos in Britain possessed any specimens was caused more by the Sakis' extremely low survival rate during importation and the first few weeks in this country. Paignton Zoo held the British longevity record for Sakis: twenty months, achieved some years before; but these monkeys are such notorious 'bad-doers' that few people risk their money attempting the almost impossible task of importing and acclimatising them to their new conditions.

Now, as I waited at the airport, I wondered if I had been wise in taking the risk. I wasn't worried about losing my money, but I was already dotty about Saki monkeys and if they were to die as a result of my importing them I should feel as if I had murdered them. I was also beginning to suffer doubts about my ability to cope with such a delicate species. If the big zoos with all their vast facilities had failed, who was I to think I stood a chance of success?

I had known from the beginning that I shouldn't be able to keep the Sakis permanently; it just wouldn't be fair with only a flat at my disposal. So as soon as I had landed in England I had sent a short note to both Paignton Zoo and to my friend Ken Smith at Exmouth Zoo (who had been Paignton's Animal Superintendent at the time they achieved the Saki record) telling them the Sakis would be for sale if they survived the journey and a short acclimatisation with me.

Ken and his wife, Trudy, telephoned me immediately from Devon, their excited voices constantly interrupting each other as they asked me to let them have the Sakis. Paignton, who also wanted them, were pipped at the post, so I promised to try to get another pair for them later if I was successful with the first ones.

Ken wanted me to send the Sakis straight down to him, without attempting to look after them myself. But I firmly vetoed the idea, as the acclimatisation was something I ardently wanted to do myself.

Now that I was actually faced with the moment of taking charge of the Sakis at the airport, I was almost inclined to think it would be wiser just to give them a meal and a rest and then put them on the train for Exmouth.

A uniformed official put his head around the door. 'You can come and see them now,' he said kindly. I followed him through the lofty freight shed to the small specially-heated animal-room. As we went through the door we were met by the raucous sounds of monkey-chatter and parrot squawks. I strode down through the line of crates, glancing to left and right and swiftly checking that everything was alive and well. At the far end I found the crate I was really looking for: the Saki monkeys.

I dropped to my knees and peered through the wire into the dim interior. Two furry faces gazed inquisitively back at me, one of them white, and the other brown with a yellow stripe on each cheek. I already thought of them as the Old Man and his Missus, not realising how permanently the names would stick.

I called softly to them. The female, always bashful, hunched her back and hid her face between her front legs. But the Old Man, his brown eyes alive with interest, sidled close to the wire, put out a friendly hand and gripped the finger I offered him. I sighed with relief. The first hurdle, the long air journey, had been cleared. Now for the next stage.

I had spent the weekend in a marathon session of cage-building. My spare room at home waited ready for the animals' arrival, already heated to 80° fahrenheit, the humidity increased by the use of a fine water-spray, the cages bedded with crisp wood-shavings, the bench packed with food for them: meat, eggs, milk, bread, cheese, cooked rice, various seeds and a large range of fresh fruit and vegetables.

The next step was to get the animals home as quickly as possible, put them into the larger cages, give them a good meal and allow them to sleep off their travel weariness. I had hired a van and driver to get me and the animals back to the flat—which was in a country house not far away. Once there, the driver helped me up the stairs with the crates.

My first job was to move all the crates into the heated spare room and push some food through the wire fronts to take the edge off the animals' appetites while the long job of uncrating and re-caging was started. This couldn't be done haphazardly. First I had to decide which cage was most suitable for each batch of animals—no easy task when accommodation was so limited. Unlike future consignments, the contents of which were just guesswork until they actually arrived, at least this first time I had known exactly what was coming. So I already had a mental plan of how to allot the cages and I had had them fitted ready with the right-sized perches and suitable water-dishes.

Next I had to make up my mind about the order of unpacking. With large consignments, unpacking and simultaneous feeding often took me six or eight hours, so it was vital to get the neediest animals into comfortable quarters early on.

Priority could be decided only at the last moment, since so many factors had to be taken into account. Any animal

144

showing signs of distress, which was fairly rare, was always unpacked and tended immediately, being given extra warmth and, where possible, dosed with a solution made up of whisky, honey, aqueous vitamins and terramycin.

Baby animals always had a high priority in unpacking, as did small birds like tanagers, and very special priority was given to species that were known to be delicate. The remainder were unpacked as they came, with snakes always left to last, although I placed their crates close to the fire so that they could regain the body heat they had lost during the long journey.

With my first consignment of animals there was never any doubt which animals would receive the highest priority in unpacking. The Sakis were going to have the best of everything. I had already prepared a dish of food for them. Having been in Guyana myself, I had the luck to know the staple diet that the natives would have fed to any captured animals: egg, milk and minced beef to the carnivorous mammals, and bananas and cooked rice to the rest, including most of the birds. I could avoid digestive upsets in the animals by feeding them the same diet and introducing more nutritious ingredients only in small but increasing quantities. As well as cooked rice and bananas, the Sakis' diet soon contained tiny amounts of apple, pear, cucumber, orange, carrot, lettuce, swede, cabbage, stale bread, raisins, nuts, sweet biscuits, parrot seed, oats, hardboiled egg, minced meat and cheddar cheese.

A lot of my success in a high-survival rate amongst the animals from South America lay in a slow change-over of diet, and the rest I attribute to my use of Abidec, a multivitamin solution made for human babies, which I added, in increasing quantities, to the food of all the mammals and birds. For a long time I had a blind faith in Abidec, although its effects could be estimated only in a negative form by my losing so few animals. But later I was able to demonstrate its near-magical properties in a positive form.

The Saki cage was now ready. Their crate was not easy to take apart; nor, I was to discover, were any of Mr Low's crates, as the lids were invariably fastened down with dozens of long nails. It was a sometimes painful and always time-consuming task.

After the lids were off the next step was often even more time-consuming: getting the animals into the cage. It would have been a fairly simple job to catch them by hand and move them, but I am very much against this with mammals unless it cannot be avoided. Forcible handling, however gentle, is bound to give them another shock at a time when they are already nervous and upset, particularly monkeys who passionately resent being picked up. So with the great majority of animals I held the crate against the open cage door and allowed them to move voluntarily. Sometimes it took a great deal of patience, and a stiff, hunched back that wouldn't straighten for another half-hour, but the results were worth it. Many times that winter I longed for some large walk-in pens where I could leave the opened crates, allowing the occupants to take their time about emerging, while I could get on with more important things.

The Sakis were no trouble at all. The Old Man walked into the cage without any hesitation, gave it a quick and presumably favourable inspection, and then came back to fetch his mate. She looked through the opening of the crate, but nervously retired again. The male looked at her in mild exasperation, then, almost shrugging his shoulders at her unreasonable timidity, he jumped over to the dish of fruit. With that most irritating of all monkey habits, he pulled all the food out of the dish for a close inspection, during which he selected the choicest morsels.

The female, watching him from the crate, could resist temptation no longer. In one quick shambling movement she joined him on the perch and with firm authority removed a grape that the Old Man was clutching in his hand. He glared at her ludicrously and seemed about to argue, but it was already too late. She was munching ponderously, grape juice dribbling down her chin, and daintily using her fingers to remove the skin from her mouth. He turned again to the dish and picked up the only other grape. Again the female whisked it out of his hand before he could get it to his mouth. This time he gave a high-pitched exclamation of annoyance: 'Chk-chk-chk.'

Still standing there holding the crate over the open door, I couldn't help giving a chuckle of amusement. The monkeys reacted instantly, giving a moving display of their relationship which I had first witnessed in Georgetown. The Old Man ran to the wire front of the cage, gripped it with his hands and shook it furiously like a miniature enraged gorilla, his voice rising up the scale: 'Chrrrrrrrrrrr.'

Having made his displeasure with me plain, he dashed back to the female. Meanwhile she had tried to disassociate herself from any danger or unpleasantness by slowly humping her back until her head was between her front legs and hidden by her heavy cape of fur. All that her perch now held was a large and very shaggy round ball of hair, looking not unlike some of the brown wasp- and ant-nests in the trees in Guyana. I was to find that all female Sakis would behave like this.

The Old Man hugged her and, chattering softly, managed to persuade her slowly to unroll again. Now and then he would look across at me and swear mildly, as if saying, 'See what you've done!' He put his arm possessively around her shoulders, but she kept giving me quick nervous glances and hastily looking away again when she saw that I was still watching. The Old Man shifted his arm so that his hand rested on top of her head with his fingers splayed over her eyes so that she need not see me. Then, for the second time in our acquaintance, so that I knew it was no accident, he bent his head and kissed her cheek, very slowly and affectionately. At the same time his eyes gazed at me, in a mute but expressive plea for me to be kind to her.

As I backed away very quietly and closed their cage door, I already realised that to know Sakis was to fall in love with one of Nature's most enchanting creatures. Ken and Trudy Smith would have to wait a while before I handed them over. I was going to complete their acclimatisation myself.

Sakis are so different from other monkeys in character, movement and appearance, that I can hardly consider them in the same context. Their coats are thick and heavy, particularly the long cape of coarse hair over their shoulders. The female is a rather dull brown, but the male is black with a sprinkling of silver. Both have very long tails, which are exceptionally densely furred with stiff curly hair, so that they are often six or more inches wide down their whole length. The tail hangs down straight when a Saki sits on a perch, and a very impressive sight it is. But I have often thought what a cumbersome appendage it must be to them in the wild, tangling with the tree-top twigs, catching on thorns and razor-grass.

The male's face was white and short-furred, while the female's was brown with a slanting yellow streak on each cheek. The long hair on their heads was parted almost symmetrically down the middle, and both had fringes over their foreheads, more pronounced and ragged in the female. One odd detail that I noticed in them and other individuals since was a minute protuberance on the bridge of their noses between the eyes, pale-coloured and very much resembling a clinging tick. That's just what I thought they were at first, but they were permanent if puzzling appendages, hardly noticeable except on close inspection.

Their voices were quite unlike those of any other monkeys of a similar size, the trill being more reminiscent of a squirrel-monkey or marmoset. Ordinary conversational tones were a bird-like twitter, but when the Old Man was annoyed his voice altered to a sharp and abrupt sound: 'Chk-chk-chk,' like a cog-wheel turning. Real anger was indicated by a different cry: 'Chrrrrrrrrrr,' which started low, rose to the top of the scale, broke off and started again. Only the male ever gave these two cries of displeasure; the female would curl herself into a silent ball if anything worried her.

Their movement was extraordinarily interesting and distinctive from other species of monkeys. When on the ground they never walked on all fours; their normal mode of travel was a series of kangaroo-hops with their hind legs, using their hands only to balance themselves by lightly touching the floor at each bound. But sometimes the male would walk upright on his hind legs, usually with his arms held loosely, but occasionally he held them high above his head like a gibbon.

As I unpacked and fed all the other animals I paused often to gaze at the Sakis, now affectionately offering each other tit-bits of food. Cornflakes and peanuts were particularly popular, although I kept their apparently favourite food, grapes, to the minimum at first so that their bowels should not be loosened. I knew I should have to let them go one day, because I had promised them to Ken, but meanwhile I felt a conviction, based on nothing more specific than my devotion to Sakis, that I could bring them through the first difficult weeks myself.

Most of the animals were in the flat for only a few days before they were sent on to zoos and bird-farms. The exceptions were the Sakis, who eventually stayed six weeks with me, and a baby armadillo.

The armadillo was something of an embarrassment. It was about a foot long and nearly as wide, and I had bought it in Georgetown as a baby giant armadillo, paying a high price for it as I had an existing order from a zoo for one. It was only when I got back to England and some reference books that I discovered I had bought, not a giant armadillo, but a very similar but far less valuable thirteen-banded armadillo.

Adrian, who also lived in Cobham, was very sympathetic, since he'd made the same mistake while he was in Guyana. In fact I discovered it was the traditional *faux pas* of most zoological collectors in South America. But this was little comfort as, apart from losing a lot of money over the mistake, I was landed with a demoniac nuisance. She was docile enough during the day, curled in a fat ball and snoring loudly as she slumbered. But she made up for it at night. The armadillo was one of the noisiest and most contrary animals that I've ever had in my possession.

She seemed to resent being caged, and after noisily demolishing her dish of raw egg, minced meat and milk when she woke up in the middle of the evening, she would set off to find a way out of the detested prison. Although she was slow-witted and rather ponderous, she was possessed of remarkable persistence. Sooner or later, by lying down and pressing her armoured body against the angle of the cage and using her large front claws as pliers, the armadillo would manage to rip a hole in the wire. Once out, she caused devastation amongst the food supplies. She once smashed a lamp by pulling it off a ledge, and I was particularly nervous that she might pull the electric fire over. For such a small creature, she was extraordinarily difficult to live with, and I heaved a sigh of relief when a dealer called Bob Halpern bought her a fortnight later.

All the animals finally left for their new homes and only

the Sakis remained. Soon I would run out of the excuses for not sending them to Devon, with which I met Ken's ever-patient telephone enquiries each week. Although he received each transparently lame excuse with equanimity, I learned a long while later that Exmouth Zoo echoed with predictions of doom over my unskilled attempt to acclimatise the Sakis, particularly for the first two weeks they were in my hands. 'Wretched, wretched woman!' Trudy and Ken muttered incantations at frequent intervals. 'She'll lose them, she'll lose them!' But as the days passed, then a week, then a fortnight, and my reports on the monkeys' progress continued to be good, they gradually began to relax and believe, like me, that I really could do it.

Meanwhile, the Sakis enjoyed an almost free run of the animal-room. They spent many hours on the wide windowsill basking in the autumn sunshine. Sometimes I sat there quietly with them and they quickly learned to accept my presence. The Old Man would often rest his hand on my arm or shoulder in a companionable way. The way they thrived exceeded all my hopes. Partly, I think, it was attention to ordinary basic details, such as a high but slowly decreasing temperature, a slightly humid atmosphere, a very varied diet with particular attention to protein and vitamins, and cleanliness. But I am convinced, and Ken Smith agrees with me, that the main reason for their survival was quite simply the time and attention I gave them. Sakis like to be the centre of attention, and dote on human company. Sakis, although it may sound sentimental, want to feel loved. A few zoologists may recoil in horror at the idea, but nevertheless it is true. If a pair of Sakis were put into a first-class cage but deprived of human company except for the time necessary to give them their daily quota of top-quality food, I am certain they would die within a very short time—simply from psychological neglect. This is the only explanation I can find, and I think it is the right one, why so many big zoos have failed with Sakis while I, no more than an enthusiastic amateur, have succeeded with two groups of them. The conditions in a large zoo are almost always too impersonal for Sakis to be able to thrive. A keeper doesn't have the time, and seldom the inclination, to spend hours with just one pen of animals, talking to them, hand-feeding them, watching them closely for any sign of discomfort or fretting. I was able to do all this: I had the time and a surfeit of inclination. For hours each day I was closeted with the Old Man and his Missus, feeding them tit-bits, playing with them, improving their small but comfortable cage. The relationship between us was so close that if one of them suffered so much as a twinge of indigestion I knew about it immediately.

This personal relationship and attention continued at Exmouth where Trudy, another Saki fanatic, snaffled all the best food for them and hand-fed them such exotic trifles as chocolate cake and Smarties, which may have been bad for their teeth but were enormously good for their morale.

14

Sexing Capybaras

It could easily have all ended there, with my sinking back into a normal suburban life and digging myself another comfortable if dull rut. For although my first full-scale excursion into the zoological world—when before I had only kept a few tropical species as pets—had been of absorbing interest to me, it seemed that I just didn't have the facilities to continue it. A spare room in a flat wasn't anybody's idea of facilities, although the way the Sakis thrived proved that it had no ill-effects on the animals.

In November 1968, however, I sent for another consignment of animals from Mr Low. I had had several further enquiries from zoos and bird farms for more stock and, as I still had a capybara and some capuchins in Georgetown which Mr Low hadn't included in the last lot of animals, it seemed sensible to make up the consignment to a fair size so that I could get a reduction in the cost of air freight.

The November consignment was dispatched to me five days late, which didn't help at all with organisation. The animals arrived at Heathrow Airport without warning on a Monday morning, the same day I had invited Brian to dinner. We hadn't seen each other since our return to England and we planned to spend the evening discussing possible similar plans for the future.

Before leaving for the airport after BOAC's call to me, I galloped around getting a few things ready, particularly turning up the heat in the animal-room, for a very high temperature was essential for the animals for the first few days after importation.

As I dashed around I sent up a small prayer of thanks that the dinner-guest happened to be Brian. I knew he would certainly enjoy a busman's holiday helping me sort out the animals. I wasn't going to offer him any option, anyway!

There were innumerable delays at the airport and it was nearly four o'clock in the afternoon before I got home with the animals. They were a mixed bunch this time. Some of them were specific orders, but I had also given Mr Low a fairly free hand to use his discretion on making up the balance of the consignment, giving him a long list of the species in which I was interested. Sometimes, I was to discover, Mr Low used his discretion with brilliant results, but sometimes the results were disastrously wrong from my point of view. Mr Low did not understand that where the larger mammals were concerned I was interested only in obtaining small baby specimens, unless I specifically ordered adults. There were four good reasons for this. Whenever possible I prefer to deal with baby animals instead of adults, as on the whole they usually settle better to captivity. On the financial side baby animals are nearly always easier to sell than adults and also cost a great deal less in air-freight. But most important of all, at that time, was that I just didn't have the space or the caging to accommodate anything but very small mammals and birds, apart from a night or two in transit to a zoo with whom a sale had previously been arranged.

With this consignment Mr Low had made two bloomers. As well as two baby coatimundis, which I always welcomed, he had sent a young adult male coatimundi. I looked at it with a sinking heart. Although it was a magnificent specimen and in excellent condition, I knew I was going to have a problem: not only as far as caging facilities (and later selling) were concerned, either, but also because of the potential danger that lies in handling any male adult coati, notoriously untrustworthy animals. The fact that this one seemed to be quite tame was little consolation, for my suspicious mind quite rightly jumped to the conclusion that Sam, as I named him, had been somebody's personal pet until he turned vicious and bit his owner and was promptly sold to a dealer.

If there's one thing I'm more wary of than a wild-caught adult male coati, it's a tame coati with an unpredictable savage streak. A handler of zoo animals seldom gets hurt by the obviously dangerous animals. It's the tame ones that get you, lulling your suspicions with lengthy good behaviour until you become careless, and then attacking suddenly and for no apparent reason when you are completely off-guard. I determined to treat Sam with the utmost caution.

Mr Low's second mistake was not only costly for me but also rather tragic. I had asked for a female capybara to be sent, knowing he had a three-quarter grown one, as Twycross Zoo wanted to make up a pair with the solitary male they possessed. But Mr Low had sent two capybaras, one of which,

154

a fully grown male, had died during the air journey. A *post mortem* later revealed that it died from a brain haemorrhage, but there was no way of knowing what caused it. As a male capybara should never have been in the consignment anyway, it seemed a pitiful waste of life. The other capybara seemed healthy and in good condition, but it was impossible to see yet whether it was a female.

The baby coatis were the size of small puppies, but with ten times as much charm as any puppy I've ever met. Their fur was brindled brown and their long furry tails were ringed attractively with light and dark brown. They had high-domed foreheads, exceptionally long rubbery noses which whiffled from side to side, and a wealth of mischief in their dark eyes. Their voices were twittery squeaks, like children's rubber toys, but they managed to invest them with a wealth of different meanings: hunger, puzzlement, anger, eagerness or simple conversational chit-chat.

I was delighted to see two tame agoutis, chestnut-coloured rodents the size of a small rabbit. Their coats were smooth and glossy, they had proud Roman noses, and as their hind legs were so much higher than their front ones they always gave the impression of having their feet resting on two different levels.

They sat in my lap gnawing carrots and delighting in being petted. Already I was being bitten by the bug that gets most collectors and importers in the end, wanting to keep certain special animals instead of selling them to other people. The only real answer, of course, is to have a zoo.

Wading head-deep in crates, I continued the long job of unboxing and feeding the animals. With only a vague idea of what the consignment would contain it hadn't been possible to prepare the cages ahead of time with the correct perches and water-dishes, most of which had to be firmly fastened to prevent their being tipped over by the animals. Attending to this before uncrating each species slowed me down even more.

I had asked Mr Low to send me a wide variety of birds, and he had certainly provided a good selection. Among them were five jacanas, small and rather fragile long-legged wading birds, but unhappily three of them had died on the journey.

I unpacked the two live jacanas first and they appeared to be surprisingly perky and strong, interestedly exploring the room with dignified stilt-steps. But I discovered that as a breed they usually travel as badly as they had this time, so rather than see such a high proportion of these dainty birds die I have never again imported them by air.

All the other species of birds were quite lively and happy. There were some attractive silver-blue tanagers, a batch of wretchedly hysterical yellow-headed marsh birds—another species that I never imported again because they were so neurotic—two dozen tiny blue-wing parrotlets, rather like small pale-green budgerigars, some very smart and dapper black-and-white lined seed-eaters, and fifty violet euphonia, wren-sized birds with a lovely deep violet colour. Among the larger birds were a pair of rails, a dozen Amazon parrots, two dozen screaming conures (a type of parakeet), and a pair of sulphur-and-white-breasted toucans.

Best of all the birds, though, was a pair of small brilliantly-coloured parrots the size of blackbirds but much stockier in build. They were black-headed caiques and their colour scheme was so stunning that it was apt to stop people in their tracks when they first saw them. The cock was slightly more colourful than the hen. He had an egg-shaped black cap beginning at the base of his hooked beak and running in almost straight lines level with each eye to the nape of his neck, where the point of the cap was embellished with a small dash of green which was repeated again under each eye. His throat was pale lemon, merging into a collar of flame-orange that ran in a wide band to the back of his neck. His wings, back and upper tail were shocking green, an exotic and brilliant hue that shimmered with iridescence, shading to a deep, shot-silk blue-green on the long flight feathers. As if consciously making an effort not to run riot with the paint-box, Nature had paused and painted a restrained cream-coloured breast. But then she had another burst of enthusiasm and flourished the flame-orange brush again for the thickly-feathered thighs and underpart of the tail.

The hen bird was identical except that the orange markings were replaced with citrus yellow. It wasn't just their colour that made them such attractive birds. They were so remarkably dignified in manner compared to the larger Amazons and smaller conures. Their behaviour could be described as cool to the point of being supercilious. While the Amazons and conures squabbled for their food like participants in a rugby scrum, the caiques stared with profound gravity at their dish of fruit before making their final selection. The piece of fruit was delicately transferred to one foot, the claws holding it skilfully while the food was slowly eaten in small beakfuls.

The Amazons and conures were uninhibited, screaming and cackling, arguing and fluttering in excessive energy, while the caiques sat stiffly to attention on their perch, silent and disapproving as they contemplated the behaviour of their ill-mannered cousins. The only time they showed faint signs of positive agitation was if I approached them closely or reached a hand into their cage. Even then their reaction was somehow in keeping with their usual dignified demeanour. Almost any bird if it is nervous will flutter off the perch in order to escape your unwelcome attentions. But these two merely puffed up their feathers and slowly *leaned* backwards as my hand approached, until sometimes their stance seemed to defy gravity, and then they straightened and leaned forward, always in unison, as I withdrew my hand. I could slowly wave my hand backward and forward, and as if there was a piece of string attaching us the two birds would lean back and forth at the same time. The next day I heard Adrian continually cursing as he tried to photograph them, for they leaned in accordance to the proximity of the camera, which had a close-up lens, and it was almost impossible to get them into focus for more than a split second.

The only sound I had so far heard the caiques make was a low churring noise of warning when I approached them too closely. As I continued with the unpacking I began to think that, unlike all other species of parrots, these two were going to be nice, quiet and well-behaved birds. Their real cry, when it came, was so unexpected and out of character that, having my back close to them at that moment, I almost leaped out of my skin. The cry was raucous and wildly flamboyant, a cross between a seagull and a farmyard cockerel. 'Yak-a-HOOOOOOOO!' the cry resounded, almost shattering the windows. The effect was startling. I spun round to stare dis-believingly at them, but they were already settling down their feathers after their brief burst of emotion and merely stared back at me with expressions of arrogant disdain.

Brian, my unwary dinner-guest, arrived at six-thirty, as I was finishing uncrating some birds.

'Don't just stand there,' I greeted him. 'Take off your coat and come and help!' As I had anticipated, Brian was more than willing. He was deeply interested in animals, especially in their behaviour, and like me he soon discovered the tremendous excitement of receiving a consignment of animals, particularly when its contents are largely unknown until the moment of arrival. I know of no excitement quite like it, and although I suppose it was remarkably unbusiness-like of me I was like a child who'd received a sackful of mystery prizes. Some were booby prizes, like Sam the adult coati, others were just what I wanted, like the Amazons and baby capuchins, and yet others were undreamed of delights, like the caiques and a charming little red-handed tamarin which I hadn't yet had time to unpack.

For the first few minutes Brian was torn in several different directions. It was the first time he had seen my Saki monkeys. Sakis were a special interest of his but, like me, the only live ones he'd seen before were a pair in Georgetown Zoo in Guyana. Brian gazed at the Old Man and his Missus with an expression approaching exaltation on his face. The female curled up at the sight of a stranger and the Old Man did his enraged-gorilla-shaking-the-bars act, followed by a tender kissing session with his wife.

At that stage I'd had the Sakis for four weeks and my success meant almost as much to Brian as it did to me, for we hoped it was the first few steps on the path that would one day lead to breeding Sakis in captivity. This, as far as we could ascertain, had only been achieved by one zoo in the world. So strong is the spell that Sakis cast that Brian seemed mesmerised as he watched them. To wake him up again I drew his attention to the tamarin and he fell upon its crate with cries of delight. Dragging him away from the tamarin at last, I set him to work helping me move a batch of Amazon parrots out of their crate and into a cage. 'There's a leather

158

glove somewhere,' I told him, as the birds would have to be lifted out by hand. 'Oh, I won't bother with gloves,' he dismissed the idea casually.

Ask any zoo-man which species he has most often been bitten by and I'll lay odds-on it will be parrots. Not just once or twice, but continually. In between times it's so easy to forget the excruciating pain of getting your fingers trapped in a parrot's powerful beak; and seldom is there a scar to provide a permanent reminder. Add to this the parrot's harmless appearance, when meanwhile the intrepid zoo-man has been handling far bigger and potentially really dangerous animals, and it's easy to see why he persists in picking up wild parrots with his bare hands. He very soon remembers, though, as the vice-like grip of a heavy beak tightens around a defenceless finger. The worst part is that the blighters just won't let go, and as the mandibles inexorably grind closer it's easy to understand why thumbscrews were such an effective method of torture a couple of centuries ago. The person who invented them had undoubtedly had an experience with a parrot.

I was standing ready to manipulate the cover of the crate and the door of the cage as Brian shifted the parrots over. He picked up the first one, clasping his hands firmly around its body. I closed the crate-lid and opened the cage door. Instead of immediately putting the bird inside, Brian started to bend slowly over with a most peculiar expression on his face. The attitude (slowly buckling) and the expression (quiet and wordless agony) was one I was soon to know well and recognise instantly, and which, coining a terrible pun, I was to dub 'a bout of parrot-vice'. But that first time I just stared in surprise at Brian and asked worriedly, 'Are you all right?' I thought maybe he had acute indigestion. The answer came as a whisper through clenched teeth, carried on a slow outward breath: 'He's–got–my–thumb.'

I came to the rescue, forcing the bird's great beak open and releasing Brian's by now multi-coloured thumb. I gripped the parrot round the neck and with Brian still holding its body we began to move it towards the open cage door.

Half-way there parrot-vice struck me. Slowly I started to buckle, and seeing the strange and rather wild look on my face Brian, like I had been, was puzzled. 'What's wrong?' he

159

asked. 'He's–got–my–bloody–thumb–now,' I breathed.

After Brian had rescued me we almost threw the wretched bird into the cage. Then, like a couple of kids with lollipops, we sat down on some crates and sucked our mangled thumbs in thoughtful silence.

After a few minutes it was time to start work again. 'Where did you say the gloves were?' Brian asked. Even with thick leather gloves protecting us it was a finger-bruising task. When it was over we had a quick cup of coffee to help us recover and during this time Brian asked me what was in a closed crate placed near the fire.

'Boa constrictors,' I replied. His face lit up, for he was particularly interested in snakes. 'Can I get them out now?'

'No,' I said unkindly, 'snakes always come last after all the other animals. It'll be a special treat for you after helping me finish the rest of the work.'

Even without coercion, I doubt if I could have prevented Brian from helping. 'By the way,' I told my long-suffering dinner-guest, 'if you get hungry help yourself to some of the animals' fruit supplies off the shelf.' (We never did get any dinner. It ended with cold meat sandwiches at midnight and Brian sleeping on the sofa with my two cats pulling the blankets off him with unquenchable *joie de vivre*!)

Adrian arrived at half past eight that evening to collect the corpse of the dead capybara to take it for *post mortem*. He was studying for his BSc degree in zoology at college and had the facilities, the experience and the willingness to do such jobs for me. I got a free *post mortem* and he got a free skeleton and pelt to help build up his scientific collection.

'Do you know you can hear that lot right out on the road?' Adrian observed as I let him in. There was a hundred-metre long driveway to the road. Now that I stopped to listen, I realised that the noise was indeed somewhat excessive. The parrots and conures screeched non-stop, the other birds added their quota of noise, and the various monkeys, twenty of them counting the Sakis, howled, squealed, yodelled and yelped.

With Adrian recruited to help us, the work progressed rapidly. We had already uncrated the twelve squirrel monkeys and I wasn't too pleased with them. They had obviously been kept in bad conditions before being freighted, being thin and quarrelsome, with very dirty coats and a number of old and new bites on them. I should have to keep the worst ones for several weeks before they were in a fit enough condition to sell. Luckily none of them had enteritis, a disease frequently and fatally contracted by monkeys kept in bad conditions. The capuchins, however, were a sound bunch, three babies and a trio of adults that I intended to send by air to Dublin Zoo the following afternoon.

To my surprise the male Saki was intensely jealous of any attentions I paid to the other monkeys, particularly the big capuchins. He chittered with annoyance, shook the wire and performed frenzied acrobatics to draw my attention to him. I was very flattered and assured him I still loved him and the Missus best.

While Adrian and I had been uncrating the big capuchins, Brian had been converting one of the large empty crates to serve as a temporary cage for the tamarin and was now hand-feeding her with slices of banana. His long, lanky form was concertinaed uncomfortably down in front of the cage, but he had an utterly absorbed expression as he fed the tiny creature, only eight inches high with a face no bigger than a penny.

She was like a gentle old lady at a tea-party, well-bred but perhaps a little shy, and ever so slightly flirtatious with the men. She sat there dressed in good-quality black furs and, incongruously, elbow-length ginger-red gloves, accepting slices of banana from Brian as daintily as though they were thinly-cut cucumber sandwiches. Each time he offered her a fresh slice she gave a faint half-hearted twitter to indicate that really she shouldn't, it was too greedy of her. But she needed little persuasion. Each time she accepted another slice she let her tiny paw rest in Brian's hand rather longer than was necessary while she gazed coyly into his eyes. I felt I could hardly refuse when Brian asked if he could buy her to give to Gerald Durrell in Jersey, and I willingly agreed to keep her for about a fortnight while he arranged her transport.

We had left the two most difficult animals until last: Sam, the big coati, and the three-quarters grown capybara. We prepared the largest of the wire-fronted crates for Sam and were well-armed with sticks when we transferred him, for

161

none of us were very convinced by his air of friendliness. Apart from the power of coatimundis' long jaws, their attack is particularly dangerous because of their ability to cling limpet-like with all four legs and their habit of continually savaging their victim instead of biting once and then retiring. Ken Smith was one of the people I knew who'd been attacked by coatis. In his case it was two at once, late at night when he was alone in his zoo. One of them clung to his leg and buried its teeth in his thigh, and the other got his arm and started savaging his shoulder. His injuries were serious, and it was only by using all his strength that he was able to tear both animals off him and get out of their cage.

Sam's behaviour was exemplary when we moved him. His complete lack of fear showed that he had obviously been somebody's personal pet until quite recently, and his magnificent condition indicated that he had been very well cared for.

Then we came to the capybara. The only cage I had free was a large two-compartment dog kennel affair. It would be adequate for one or two nights, and if the animal was a female I had no problem, as I could rail it to Twycross Zoo the next day. But if it was a male I should have almost as much difficulty selling it as I was going to have with Sam.

There is something very endearing about capybaras. They are the world's largest rodent, with an adult male standing about twenty-one inches at the shoulder, measuring four feet in length and weighing over a hundred pounds. They are very like a giant golden-brown guinea-pig, with a very broad body, short legs and a large head with a blunt, squared-off face that always bears an expression of affable stupidity. Our one was just under one metre long and weighed perhaps fifty pounds. This was the first of the species that I had ever handled and I wasn't quite sure what to expect. I had heard that capybaras in captivity become delightfully tame, but there was no way of knowing how recently this one had been caught, or how much aggression it might display. The massive jaws, equipped with sharp rodent's teeth, looked capable of chopping off one of our arms at the shoulder. It seemed wise to treat the animal with preliminary caution.

We fixed things so that the animal could walk out of its crate and into the cage without being forcibly handled. As

162

the question of its sex was of burning importance to me, we all crouched down and ill-manneredly tried to peer under its belly as it slowly walked the few steps into its cage. But the capybara was so fat and its body so low to the ground that even with our heads pressed to the floor it was impossible to see the relevant parts of its anatomy. It was now nearly midnight and I was so tired that my knees were trembling after the exertion of eight hours' continuous crouching and bending over crates and cages. I shrugged and closed the capybara's door; I'd return later for a sexing session, when I had a bit more strength. All the animals had been caged and fed now, except for the box of snakes, at which Brian was casting longing glances. I suggested he take it into the sitting-room where there was more room to unpack it, while I made some coffee and sandwiches.

By the time I brought the food into the sitting-room, Brian and Adrian had un-nailed the snake box. There were three boas, ranging in length from five to seven feet. We took one each and sat down with a sandwich in one hand and a snake in the other, examining them carefully for any abrasions or mouth canker. After a while, as the boas seemed fairly docile, we released them and allowed them to glide slowly and elegantly around the floor.

After we finished the sandwiches I decided I just had to know the sex of the capybara if I was going to get any sleep that night. Adrian offered to come and help me and we left Brian in charge of catching and boxing the snakes. Ours was a difficult job. The dog kennel was at ground level, with a full-width door to each of the two compartments, which were connected inside by a foot-wide open gap. It wasn't the best of cages to hold any animal that decided to charge us while we had the doors open. I considered the problem, while the capybara gazed at me with a foolish expression on its large flattened face. Then I gave Adrian a pair of leather gloves and, in case of emergency, a hefty stick to protect himself; he needed them more than I did—he was going to be on the biting end. I gently chivvied the capybara until it had the front half of its body in the compartment Adrian was guarding and its rear half in my side of the cage. If the animal charged forward when I touched it, Adrian would try to hold it back as best he could, but if it started biting he was to let it go and scramble clear.

As it still proved impossible to answer the vital question by getting down low and looking, I very carefully slid my hand under the capybara's belly to try to sex it by touch. At my first indecent touch the capybara sat down hurriedly. At the same time, Adrian told me from his side of the cage, a look of shocked horror flitted over its stupid face.

With fifty pounds of capybara on my hand there was little I could do except withdraw it and coax the animal to stand up again, while Adrian kept close to its head to prevent its bolting forward. Each time I tried to slide my hand underneath, the capybara reacted the same way by collapsing its heavy bottom on top of my hand. We paused for a moment to ease our cramped legs and backs. Then I worked out another tactic. Adrian gallantly agreed to hold the capybara firmly around the neck. Then, casting delicacy aside, I caught hold of the animal's hind legs and lifted them high so that I could take a proper look. To my great satisfaction I had established that the long-suffering beast was indeed a female.

She was, in fact, extremely docile, an amiable if rather dim-witted creature, and our careful precautions for our safety were quite unnecessary. The trouble with newly-arrived animals is never being sure for a few days whether they are safe or dangerous to handle. It makes you feel a bit foolish when such careful precautions turn out to be needless, and this in turn sometimes makes you less careful with the precautions you take with the next animal, which may well turn out to be really dangerous.

We stroked the capybara to soothe her feelings and fed her some more carrots and lettuce. Then I dimmed the lights a little to let the tired animals sleep, leaving a medium light burning all night so that the birds could continue feeding as long as they liked. A whispering, rustling peace had descended on the room as we crept out.

15
Sexy Sam

COATIMUNDI

The next couple of days saw the clearance of most of the animals to zoos, bird-farms and dealers. I was then left with a couple of Amazons, a few of the marsh birds, the six worst squirrel monkeys whose condition I had to improve before selling them, the tamarin that I was looking after for Brian, Sam, the adult coati. and, of course, the Sakis.

My problem of what to do with Sam until I sold him was quickly solved when Janine telephoned me from her boarding kennels in Sussex to have a chat. When I bewailed my difficulties over accommodating Sam, Janine immediately offered to board him for me. She had one of the big cat-houses empty, which contained a row of eight-feet-square pens wired with heavy chain-link mesh. One of these would be ideal for Sam and she would be able to fix up an overhead fire to keep him warm.

Although eager to accept her offer, I tried to impress on her that Sam was potentially dangerous and would need cautious handling. He seemed very tame, but he was already showing a streak of stubbornness that made me think he would have little hesitation in using his teeth if he couldn't get his own way. But Janine was still keen to have him. She was a good dog- and cat-handler and now she was enthusiastic to try her hand with zoological stock.

'I'm 'appy to look after anyzing for you, except snakes or monkeys,' she offered cheerfully.

The next day I drove down to Hassocks with Sam snorting with rage inside a crate. When we arrived at the boarding kennels, Janine and I carried the box inside the cat-house. We took the crate into one of the pens, already prepared with sawdust, straw and an overhead fire. After consultation we decided we should have to lock ourselves inside the pen with Sam as we released him from the crate, but armed ourselves with thick sticks just in case of trouble.

As soon as I loosened the lid Sam erupted from it like a high-pressure water-spout. With high-pitched squeaks he ran around the pen, inspecting every inch of it, dashing up the walls, climbing upside down across the wired ceiling and down the other side. At frequent intervals he stopped to rub his scent glands hurriedly on different objects, marking out his territory.

166

Then he bounced over to me, squeaking in a friendly fashion. I kept still and he rubbed himself against my legs affectionately. Then he wrapped his arms around one of my legs. I didn't much like the power of his grip, still being very distrustful of his temperament, so I flicked his long rubbery nose gently with the stick and made him let go.

He glared at me and, an action we were to come to know well, started rapidly chopping his teeth together as a sign of displeasure. But his irritation was short-lived and he decided to go and introduce himself to Janine. She was wearing a pair of knee-length boots and at first Sam was intrigued by the shininess of the leather and its smooth feel as he rubbed against her. Then, with no warning at all, he suddenly charged up one of her legs and vanished inside her skirt, only his long plushy tail dangling below the hemline like a bell-pull. Very sensibly, Janine froze into immobility, although her face showed the strain of enduring his exploratory travels.

'Get 'im off me!' she breathed.

I crouched down to help, but found myself in rather a predicament. I did not like the idea of lifting her skirt at the edge and walloping whatever part of Sam I could find with the stick; he might well retaliate by burying his teeth in Janine's thigh. I temporarily prevaricated by assuring Janine with hearty confidence that I had the situation well under control.

'I don't care what you 'ave under control,' she hissed back at me, 'but I 'ave a vairy sexy animal under my skirt. Get 'im off!'

The only thing I could think of was to give Sam's dangling tail a small tug. It hardly seemed the drastic action the situation called for, but to my astonishment it worked. There was a shrill twitter of protest from somewhere in the region of Janine's hip and then her skirt bulged as Sam somersaulted and came head-first back down her leg to investigate the impudence of someone pulling his tail. I rapped his nose sharply with the stick and he immediately let go of Janine and approached me threateningly, his teeth chopping and gnashing together angrily. Using our sticks to push him away from us, we backed to the door and out of it.

Once outside, Janine let out her breath, which I think she'd been holding since Sam first disappeared up her skirt.

'My God!' she said feelingly. 'Does 'e often do zat?'

'I don't know,' I said truthfully. 'I always wear long trousers.'

The coati, eager to have our attention again, leapt on to the wire beside us and stuck a friendly paw through the mesh.

'Listen to me, Sexy Sam,' Janine told him sternly, 'you kindly remember in future zat we don't 'ave goings on like zat 'ere!'

The name Sexy Sam stuck, especially as he quickly fell in love with a mop that was usually propped in the passageway of the cat-house. Janine started to let him out into the passage each day when she was cleaning his pen, and as well as rushing joyously up and down he frequently displayed embarrassingly amorous attentions towards the mop. Furthermore, if he saw anyone touch it he became almost hysterical, scrabbling and biting at the wire of his pen as he tried to come to the mop's protection.

Janine telephoned me daily with reports on the coati's progress, while meanwhile I wrote to dozens of zoos trying to sell him. Janine's increasing confidence in Sam worried me, for she soon became convinced that he was quite tame and I was sure he was untrustworthy when it came to a clash of wills. Each time she telephoned I cautioned her not to trust the coati too far.

One morning her normally lively voice was subdued when I answered the telephone. 'Zat terrible animal 'as bitten me,' she admitted.

It had happened as she was returning Sam to his pen after cleaning it out. He started to go in quite willingly, but with no warning suddenly wheeled round, grabbed her leg with all four of his, and buried his teeth in her ankle. There was a small boy at the end of the passage, her kennel-maid's son, and Janine was scared to think what would happen if Sam attacked him. The risk meant that she couldn't try to beat Sam off her leg where she was in the passage, and at that moment there was nobody else on the isolated property.

Shouting to the boy to lock himself in one of the nearby pens, Janine managed to reach the mop a few yards away,

168

dragging her leg with the coati still clinging to it and savaging her ankle. She staggered back to the open door of Sam's pen and then clouted him across the back with the mop's wooden handle. He immediately released his grip on her and she slammed the door shut on him as he came at her again, his teeth chopping furiously.

Her ankle was badly mangled, but with far more deep bruising than torn skin. Although she disinfected it immediately and took some antibiotic pills, the bite turned septic and she was limping badly for several weeks.

She treated Sam with far more caution now, but bore me not the slightest grudge for my animal having mauled her. Both of us were faintly relieved when three weeks later Manchester Zoo said they'd be delighted to buy Sam as a mate for their lonely female coati. The fact that he wasn't safe to handle wasn't important to them and they were only too pleased to obtain such a splendid specimen at the low price I offered. So off Sam went to Manchester, where he was soon making ardent love to the female coati, which I'm sure he found more satisfying than the mop.

The day came towards the end of November when at last the Sakis had to leave. I had realised that if I didn't send them down to Exmouth now I would never be able to part with them. I had, after all, done what I set out to do. The Sakis had been with me for six weeks and were now so full of health that they had every chance of surviving for a very long time in captivity. As a result, my confidence in my ability to keep really delicate animals had increased greatly.

In no small way my success with the Sakis made me turn more serious consideration to the dream that was lurking at the back of my mind: to take a large jungle island in Guyana and turn it into a wildlife sanctuary cum zoo-without-bars, where all the animals, although artificially fed, would live entirely free.

The fact that South American wildlife is invariably extremely difficult to observe in its natural state, mainly because the animals are so shy, is frequently the source of great disappointment to visitors. And yet the forests are filled with a fascinating range of animals, of greater zoological interest than any other country in the world; at the same time they have been

169

little studied by the experts, again largely due to the difficulties of observing them in the wild.

Yet the capuchins that escaped from us when I was living on the island in the Essequibo River had completely lost their shyness and timidity, although they had been captured in the wild only four weeks beforehand. Instead of bolting away from humans, like the capuchins on the mainland, they stayed willingly within sight but just out of reach, cavorting in the trees around camp and taking the food I put out for them until at last they were re-caught.

The seed was sown in my mind. If that had worked unintentionally with capuchins, what other species of monkeys would it work with intentionally, keeping them penned in a similar way for a few weeks before release? The possibilities were endless: squirrel monkeys, woollies, spiders, Saki monkeys, tamarins, marmosets, uakaris, red howler monkeys.

I turned my mind to other types of animals: deer, capybara, tapir, paca, coatimundi, otter, agouti. All of these would need taming from babies, gradually being given the full run of the island, as wild adult specimens would simply swim away at the first opportunity.

The birds—so many hundreds of fascinating species that my mind boggled at the thought of them—could be preconditioned in one of three ways: some, like parrots and trumpeters, could be tamed from fledglings; large birds, like flamingoes, cranes and macaws, could have their wings clipped for one season in the hope that by the time their flight feathers had regrown they would be reluctant to leave the free food supplies; and yet other birds, like tanagers and humming-birds, where neither wing-clipping nor taming were feasible, could be carefully homed from an aviary.

Predators were the only species that would have to be confined, but I envisaged very large natural enclosures for them, filled with trees and boulders and a stream. Puma, jaguar, ocelot and margay could be reared from tiny cubs on the bottle.

My mind leapt ahead to such improvements as small lakes for arapaima and manatee and giant catfish, and to a reptile house where the pens were large and naturally planted and

170

where co-habitation of the different species was concentrated upon.

Although I was almost certain I could get such an island at little or no cost from the Guyana Government, the maintenance of such a huge collection of animals would be enormous, in food, staff, boats and vehicles; for every single thing required would have to be brought perhaps a hundred miles to the island by rough track and river. So it would have to have its commercial side; a safari-lodge style hotel, I thought, with individual cabins for the visitors.

I had no doubt that it would pay. The prospect was incredibly attractive for tourists interested in wildlife photography, for this would be the only place in the world where a host of New World species obligingly kept within camera range and yet were not confined behind bars.

My mind went off on another tangent; tourists apart, what a magnificent opportunity it would be for naturalists and zoologists to make a proper study of these species in an environment that apart from artificial feeding closely approached their wild state. In such conditions the animals would almost certainly breed freely, and the sexual behaviour pattern and the rearing of the young could be easily observed and recorded from beginning to end.

This was the idea that lay at the back of my mind when I returned to England. But at first it lay quite dormant, for the probability of my tackling such an undertaking seemed as fantastic as an ordinary housewife building a moon-rocket in her back garden. The technical problems attached to such a project as mine would be overwhelming. On the zoological side alone I thought it would take me several years of study before I had sufficient knowledge to take hundreds, and perhaps thousands, of animals of different species and persuade them to share an area of two square miles of forest without either fighting, making a mass exodus, or simply failing to thrive.

But the main objection in my mind was that if the idea had been feasible then why hadn't somebody else—one of the big zoological societies—already done it? Gradually, though, I began to believe that this was simply because none of them had ever happened to live on a jungle island and seen the

171

remarkable result of an escape by comparatively newly-caught adult monkeys.

My successful acclimatisation of the Saki monkeys served to give a great boost to my self-confidence in handling animals. I began to attach less importance to text-book learning and more to practical experience and—most important of all— an unquenchable and observant interest in the individual animals.

I began to half-believe that I was capable of tackling the island project when I had the opportunity. The idea was becoming slightly more positive in my mind and I was subconsciously mulling over the innumerable potential problems, such as how to provide a monkey-free nesting ground for the birds, and how to deal with the accumulation of rotting food that would inevitably fall to the forest floor.

'Agoutis? Ants? How many needed as food scavengers?' my rough notes at that time read, jotted down on the backs of old envelopes. 'What of ant over-population? Perhaps ant-eaters or ant-birds?'

And so, like an in-calf elephant, I quietly carried my idea around with me and let it grow at its own slow pace. Saki Island Sanctuary, like an elephant foetus, couldn't be hurried.

Putting the Old Man and his Missus into a wooden box and dispatching it from Paddington Station made me feel as inhuman as if they had been children. This was getting ridiculous, I thought; I'd always prided myself on being unsentimental and, after all, the crate was warm and comfortable and the train journey fast and direct.

But just the same I chewed my nails for several hours until Ken and Trudy telephoned to say they'd arrived safely. They were volubly pleased with them, and as the Old Man and his Missus were obviously going to want for nothing in their new home there was no basis for my depression except my own sadness at parting from them.

The animal-room, although it still contained a handful of birds, the squirrel monkeys and the little tamarin, seemed very quiet and empty without the Sakis; I missed them terribly, and no longer spent most of my time in there.

Then Bob Halpern asked if I'd buy some of his surplus stock and I needed little persuasion. Apart from helping to fill the sudden gap in my life, as Halpern had bought a fair amount of animals from me in the past it seemed only fair to help him out when he was overstocked.

His van arrived with several boxes for me and within half-an-hour new life had been breathed into the silent animal-room. The only South American stock were some Gendaya conures or, as the Guyanese graphically call them, Sun Para-keets. They were indeed a sunburst of yellows and oranges. How spectacular, I thought, a great flock of them would look in a jungle island wildlife sanctuary.

I stifled the thought and carried on unpacking the boxes. There was a monitor lizard, two big brown-shouldered parrots from Zambia and three African Greys.

I'd agreed to take three monkeys, a young grivet, a baby pig-tail and a baby Hamadryas baboon. I think grivets are one of the most attractive of the common monkeys. There's a definite elegance to their long and lean bodies and their movements are as graceful and sure as a ballet dancer's. Tremendously energetic and mischievous, they are the real acrobats of the monkey world.

Jenny, as I named this one, was half-tame but not above using her teeth on the rare occasions when I had forcibly to pick her up. Her fur was short and neat, grey-green over her back and arms and an immaculate creamy-white all down her front. Her small and sharply-alert face was framed by old-fashioned sideboard whiskers that sprang in two creamy swathes of long hair from the sides of her cheeks and throat.

Sarah, the young pig-tailed monkey, was a happy extro-vert, noisy, greedy and ill-mannered. Pig-tails have been likened to chimpanzees, because of their appearance and high intelligence, but Sarah was sadly lacking in any such attraction.

Betsy the baby baboon, however, was a darling and just as much fun to have around as a baby chimp. Her face had an expression of mild but long-suffering disapproval, and it was topped with a thatch of hair which stood on end as if she'd once had a terrible fright.

Compared to Jenny, Betsy was both slow-moving and slow-witted, a fact of which Jenny was not slow to take advantage, teasing the baboon unmercifully and then leaping

173

nimbly out of her way as she ponderously tried to retaliate. But although she was not endowed with agility of mind and body, Betsy had the alternative talents of logic and mimicry. She performed slow but highly-skilled acrobatics on a rope, and without any persuasion from me taught herself to stand on her head, a pleasure that she enjoyed solemnly.

She gave an impression of passivity and, let's face it, mild stupidity and it was difficult to realise that she was like a piece of blotting paper in the way she absorbed the meaning and result of all my actions. She would quietly watch everything I did around the animal room, observing the technique of such things as the complicated and—as I thought—monkey-proof fastening on her cage door, which consisted of a series of catches and twisted wires. She never attempted to copy my actions while I was still there, but if I crept back a few minutes after leaving the animal room I would find her absorbed in the task of undoing the catches the way she had seen me do it. Whenever she was temporarily thwarted by the intricacies of some looped or twisted wire, she would sit and stare hard at it, thoughtfully scratching her head and—a particularly humanlike gesture—rubbing her nose with the back of her hand. There were few doors that defeated her in the end; the only real answer was a padlock.

She was very tame and during the eight months she was with me she never showed the slightest inclination to bite, even when she had injections. She loved to be carried around, or rather it was a case of allowing her to clasp me around the waist with her legs and arms. With her head resting comfortably against my solar plexus, she just hung on while I continued with all my jobs. As she was only fifteen inches high, she wasn't too much of a hindrance when she hitched a free lift.

Four weeks after Betsy arrived, Halpern offered to buy her back in order to sell her to a centre where they were doing behaviour-research on baboons. I was horrified at the idea, even though I knew she would have the best of physical care there. But the surroundings would be purely scientific and formal, with no relationship at all established between the humans and animals. Halpern was impatient with my refusal to sell her back. Perhaps he was right in accusing me of sentimentality, but the proposal seemed so wrong for her that I wouldn't even consider it. To me Betsy was a small child that I had temporarily adopted, and she not only needed the company and friendship of humans, but needed one human in particular to mother her and soothe her infantile feelings of insecurity. Halpern's face was a picture of ludicrous disbelief when I explained this to him.

'Why don't you buy back the pig-tail instead?' I suggested hopefully. Sarah gazed at me sourly; our mild feelings of dislike were mutual. Unfortunately he wouldn't do this.

A couple of days after Betsy and the other animals arrived, Brian came to fetch the tamarin to send it by air to Jersey. I was sorry to see her go, for she had been a gentle and attractive creature to have around the place. She was still behaving like a sweet old lady at a tea-party.

Brian was luckier on this visit; he actually got a proper meal and I didn't make him work for six solid hours as I had the last time. While he was there, however, he helped me move the two big brown-shouldered parrots into a different cage, and needless to say we were both struck by parrot-vice in the process. As their beaks were twice as large as those of Amazons, it wasn't surprising that Brian audibly questioned his wisdom in ever coming to visit me. But when he heard that another consignment of animals was due from Mr Low in the middle of December, he enthusiastically offered to come and help me when they arrived.

I had been unable to resist ordering another load of animals for two reasons. The first was that the last consignment had proved uneconomical with such a high proportion of birds in it and I had done little more than cover my costs; as I was beginning to plan some moderately sized premises to use for importing, I wanted to prove to my own satisfaction that importing would be reasonably profitable now that I knew which species were economical. Squirrel monkeys and parrots were far and away the best from a financial point of view, and they helped to cover the cost of importing the more interesting but uneconomical species, such as capybara and Sakis.

My second and most important reason for arranging another consignment of animals was that I'd had a cable from Mr Low telling me he had another pair of Sakis. Paignton

175

were still very keen to obtain a pair, and I wanted to acclimatise them to prove that my first success wasn't just a fluke.

Even more simply, and quite overwhelmingly, I wanted to have Sakis in the house again.

16

Enter Bluey, Blossom,
and Jaffa

16 December 1968 is a date I find easy to remember, partly because it heralded the arrival of a number of memorable animals, and partly because it was also the day when I developed the first mild symptoms of a deadly disease which nearly killed me some months later.

But my headache and aching limbs seemed no more than a threatening cold as I waited at Heathrow Airport for documentary clearance of the animals. I took a couple of aspirins and felt better. Brian, also, had telephoned the day before to say that he was feeling unwell and wouldn't be able to come down and help me unpack the animals, but he hoped to come and see them in a few days' time.

It was a very good consignment this time, my only immediate criticism being that Mr Low had sent me three fully-grown capuchins as well as the three baby ones I had ordered. I had asked for ten squirrel monkeys, but Mr Low had sent me twenty-five to make up for the lack of any Amazon parrots. I wasn't sure at first whether to be glad or sorry. Squirrel monkeys are profitable and this was a particularly nice bunch: clean, well-fed and healthy, with a good proportion of young ones. But I was wondering rather desperately where I was going to put them all. The existing monkeys plus the new arrivals totalled forty, and there was also a number of birds to accommodate.

Halpern came to the rescue and sent a man down the same evening to collect sixteen of the squirrel monkeys and two baby capuchins. Selling them in a large batch like this meant I received little more than half the price I would make if I sold them gradually in small quantities, but it considerably eased my accommodation problem. I was still making a reasonable profit on them, anyway, and I was left with nine very nice baby squirrel monkeys and one baby capuchin to sell gradually at higher prices.

In one of the squirrel monkey crates, discovered only when I began to un-nail it, was an unexpected baby red howler monkey. Its ugly, mournful face stared out at me and I sat back on my heels in delight. All the time I was in Guyana I had hoped to get some baby howlers, but although troupes of them were quite common along the Essequibo we had never been able to obtain any either by catching or buying.

For me, howlers come second only to Sakis in interest. They are big, morose monkeys, with heavy gleaming coats of fiery red and dark scowling faces. But although their appearance is impressive, it is really their voices that make them such remarkable animals.

We had been woken at dawn every day on the island by the chorus of howlers on the mainland. The sound, produced from a built-in echo chamber in the monkeys' throats, was so suggestive of a spirit world that it invariably made my spine tingle. The voice of a big troupe fluctuated in unison, like waves on a seashore, combining the powerful sound of drums rolling with the insubstantiality of wind blowing through a tunnel. Similes are inevitable when describing the howler chorus, for there is no other single sound like it. Some people like the sound, some hate it, but it is too emotionally disturbing for anyone ever to ignore it.

The baby howler was a sad and unsociable creature, slow-moving and timid. I never like penning a monkey on its own for they seem to need the warmth and company of other monkeys, and most importantly a participant in the absorbing social occupation of grooming each other's fur. So first I tried penning the howler with the baby capuchin that had just arrived, but the capuchin was far too rough and boisterous. Jenny and Sarah, the grivet and pig-tail, were too greedy and snatched food out of his hand all the time, and he always needed all my persuasion to make him eat.

I thought Betsy, also slow-moving and gentle, would be the answer as a companion, but she took one look at the ugly howler and started screaming as if she'd seen a bogeyman. However much I tried to coax her, she flatly refused to act as babysitter. I even tried putting two of the baby squirrel monkeys with the howler, but as the two species rigidly ignored each other there seemed little point to the arrangement and after a couple of days I took them out again so that at least I could judge how much food the howler was consuming.

A well-known zoo who had a reputation of success with delicate primates had asked me to get some howlers for them some months before, so when this baby one arrived I immediately telephoned them and they agreed to buy him. But as it

179

was so near Christmas they asked if I would keep the monkey until after the holiday. Howlers are even more notoriously difficult than Sakis. However, I agreed to the zoo's request.

The howler certainly wasn't easy, mainly because he had such a morose temperament, but having seen howlers so frequently in the wild I was convinced that the surly character and ponderous movements were ingrained characteristics. The baby howler at last began to eat what I considered a reasonable quantity of food, hanging upside down by his strongly-prehensile tail while he slowly munched; out of the great variety of foods I offered, he mostly chose banana.

He also showed a spark of vitality one day when he gave a juvenile version of the howler's chorus. It came out as an extraordinary noise, a cross between a moan, a burp and the roar of a lion caged in an echo chamber. It broke off abruptly in the middle, with the baby howler looking sulkily surprised as if he couldn't believe he was responsible for such an atrocious sound.

In his own moody way he was beginning to thrive when I sent him to the zoo eleven days later as arranged. But the zoo telephoned the next day to say the howler had died in the night. I was bitterly upset about it.

The December consignment was packed with animal personalities. There was Marnie, the male of the three adult capuchin monkeys. When I was uncrating them, with great caution for they were big monkeys which could inflict really wicked bites, I noticed that the male had a leather collar around his waist and seemed to be tame. I groaned, for if there is anything worse to handle than a tame but untrustworthy adult male coatimundi, it is a tame but untrustworthy adult male capuchin. They can not only show extreme savagery when upset, but have a great strength that enables them to cling even better than a coati and in addition have truly formidable jaws with very large canine teeth.

Male capuchins are one of the very few species that Brian treats with exaggerated respect, and I've heard him say many times, with justification, that never for a moment would he trust one or give it the chance to attack him. So when Marnie, as I called this big male, put his hand through the wire mesh of his cage and held it out appealingly to me whenever I came

180

near, I would take it obligingly enough, but as soon as he gently tried to pull my fingers nearer his teeth I would firmly pull away from his grasp. Then he would gaze at me with an expression of quiet grief because I had spurned his friendship.

He took no notice at all of the two females in the cage. His face was constantly pressed up against the wire and his soft brown eyes, filled with adoration, followed me wherever I went. One step towards him would result in his hand being held out imploringly to me. But if I put a tit-bit into it, a grape or a peanut, he would just drop it without interest; he only wanted to hold my hand.

The morning after the consignment arrived I went to give Marnie and his companions a dish of food. The door of the cage was awkwardly situated in a corner and I had to crouch down on my heels to open it, with the wall immediately on my right and another row of cages hard against my back. No sooner had I opened the door a few inches than Marnie bolted through it so fast that I never had a chance to stop him. He landed heavily in my lap and paused, staring uncertainly into my eyes, his half-open mouth showing his massive white teeth only a few inches from my face.

I was alone in the flat, and even if I were to shout I knew that no one would hear me. I wondered how on earth I was going to get him off my lap, let alone back into his cage, without getting badly bitten in the process. I was well and truly cornered, with the wall on one side, cages against my back and my knees up against Marnie's cage. The only open space was a gap eighteen inches wide to my left. But if I threw myself sideways there, the monkey would still be on top of me, and I would still have no room in which to fend him off.

It took less than two seconds for me to think all this, so that Marnie was still poised tensely on my knees when I came to the conclusion that the best thing was for me to stay quite still and see what happened. I tried to relax, although my forehead was damp and my skin tingled with apprehension. Marnie, after a moment, also relaxed. He leaned his heavy body against my chest, closed his eyes and gave a shuddering sigh as if he'd come home at last after a long, lonely journey.

His eyes flickered open again and he picked up my hand in one of his and laid it tenderly against his cheek, his eyes

181

glowing with happiness as he gazed into my face. I moved my hand very carefully and let it rest on his head a moment before I began to stroke him gently. He closed his eyes, gave a long sigh of exquisite pleasure and pressed his body tightly against me. I tried not to let all my suspicions be lulled, for although Marnie seemed such an adoring creature male capuchins were, after all, male capuchins. And my legs were beginning to suffer such agonies of cramp that I now had to try and stand up with him still clinging to me.

I shifted my left arm so that it supported Marnie's body and began to stroke him firmly with my right hand as I tried to straighten up. But the monkey's weight and my numbed legs defeated me. I had to stop stroking him and use my hand to hold on to the cage and pull myself up. Marnie gave a faint squeak of alarm and his strong arms tightened round my neck.

As I stood there for a moment, with the blood flowing painfully back into my legs, I was conscious of the capuchin's warm breath against my cheek. By now, although against my better judgement, I was almost sure that I could trust him. I walked up and down for a little while with him in my arms, showing him the other animals and the view from the window. Sometimes he would reach out and touch something gently with his long black hand, but he was very passive and well-mannered, not snatching at things as most monkeys would.

After ten minutes I felt it was time he went back into his cage, as I still had other animals to feed. This was really the crunch, for Marnie certainly didn't want to go back and if he was ever going to bite then this would be the time. I slowly lowered myself into the narrow gap in front of the cage until I was sitting on my heels. I coaxed Marnie down into my lap and opened the cage door.

'Good boy, go in,' I said firmly.

He understood. His eyes grew sad, but he didn't move. I pushed him very gently towards the open door, half-expecting him to turn on me savagely at any moment. He took my hand in both of his and slowly lifted it to his teeth. His eyes never left mine as his mouth closed over my hand, holding it as softly as a gun-dog with an egg. His great teeth didn't even prick my skin. His action was purely a demonstration to show he was equipped to hurt me if I really upset him.

'Go in, Marnie,' I insisted gently.

He let go of my hand with a sigh and walked into the cage, where he pressed his face against the wire and watched me mournfully. Who could help being utterly captivated by such a character? I never found out why he came into the hands of a dealer and I really don't think he could ever have bitten anyone, for although he would always place his teeth over my hand when he was displeased with me, he never once even grazed the skin, and my firm insistence on obedience always won the day.

During the following days I often let Marnie accompany me around the rest of the flat. In the evenings Pinto, my poodle, found herself ousted from her accustomed position in my lap as I watched television. Marnie's big body overflowed my lap and his muscular arms hugged me while his head rested on my shoulder. Sometimes we would sit together on the rug in front of the fire, with Marnie stretched out in abandoned poses with closed eyes and making soft chukking sounds of contentment as I groomed his fur with my fingers.

I didn't want to sell Marnie to a zoo, for I felt he needed more human love than he was likely to get there. Neither did I have the space to keep him permanently, much as I would have liked to. My problem was solved a week later when a local man came along with the intention of buying a baby squirrel monkey as a pet. The attraction between him and the capuchin was immediate and mutual. Marnie sat in his arms for half-an-hour stroking the man's beard with an expression of wonder and soft cooing sounds of delight.

I would never normally consider selling an adult capuchin to a member of the public, but not only was Marnie an exceptional capuchin but also the man was exceptionally intelligent and sensible. He had kept monkeys successfully before, and fully understood my warnings about the expense of feeding him, the danger if Marnie ever bit, and the importance of avoiding a serious clash of wills with the monkey which might result in an attack.

The squirrel monkeys were forgotten. Marnie and he wanted each other. When the man drove off at last he had one hand on the steering wheel and one holding Marnie's

183

hand which was thrust through the wire door of a crate. I'm glad to say that their relationship has continued to be a great success, with Marnie a deliriously happy and honoured member of the family, with his own bedroom and a wire run in the garden for summer days.

Although Mr Low had unfortunately been unable to obtain any Amazon parrots for me, there were a pair of military macaws, two very young blue-headed parrots and five black-headed caiques.

There was never really any doubt that I would keep the two blue-headed parrots, for when I opened their crate they immediately walked up my arm in a most proprietory manner. They were in the middle of shedding their fledgling feathers and growing their adult plumage and they presented a very tattered appearance, with feathers and feather-stubs sticking out at all angles. Every time they shook themselves, clouds of tiny feathers filled the air around them.

One was much more colourful than the other, with a deep blue head which shaded into violet around the neck and the top of the breast, the rest of him being a rather dull green except for the shading of blue and red underneath the tail. I naturally took this bird to be the cock. I named him Bluey and my estimate of his sex seemed confirmed by the fact that he was so tame and friendly, whereas the other bird, which I named Blossom, was rather more shy and followed only where Bluey led. Blossom had the same markings, but the colour over her head was much paler and less defined than with Bluey.

When they both eventually produced adult plumage, however, their coloration was identical and it was several months later when I realised from their courting behaviour that in fact Bluey was the hen and Blossom the cock. I still refer to them and think of them by their original names and sex, though; it makes life simpler.

The third character to become a permanent member of the family at that time was a baby male caique. I had professed a wish for a baby caique when I first saw the species in November, and here to my delight were three babies with their parents. I picked out a little cock bird for my own and sold the others.

184

Jaffa, as I called him, was literally right out of the nest and I had to hand-feed him for the first few days. Young caiques are not very easy to rear, being among the most delicate species of the hardy parrot family, and I nearly lost him twice from sudden chills during the next few months. Each time I just managed to save him by giving a very high degree of warmth and oral doses of Abidec and terramycin.

He is sitting on my shoulder as I write, pulling out my hair strand by strand with great concentration, at two years old a strong and healthy bird with an extravagant colour scheme and a rumbustious personality.

I had really been attracted to the idea of keeping a caique because of the ultra-dignified behaviour of the adults. But Jaffa has never known the meaning of dignity. He's the craziest bird I've ever met, a real whizz-kid of a parrot, always busy, always bustling and interfering with everything. I thought perhaps Jaffa would acquire a little dignity and passivity as he matured, but if anything he gets worse as he gets older. He fizzes with activity from the time he wakes up until the time I cover his cage at night, swinging, climbing, flapping and scurrying, cackling and whistling cheerfully all the time and occasionally splitting the air with his seagull-cockerel cry of: 'Yak-a-HOOOO!'

His behaviour contains many oddities which I have never seen in other birds. He will frequently hang from a perch with one claw, spinning slowly and screeching all the time as if he is stuck and can't rescue himself. I know better now than to waste my time helping him back on to the perch, for he will just give me an impatient look and start doing the same thing all over again.

Another favourite trick, which always brings innocent visitors rushing to his rescue, is hanging from the perch with the tip of his hooked beak and pedalling the air very slowly with his legs as if he is in the last stages of exhaustion and too weak to climb up and too frightened to drop down. But his oddest and most persistent habit is lying on his back on the floor of the cage, sometimes juggling a plaything in his claws, sometimes just lying there at ease with his legs sticking up, apparently deep in thought, and sometimes rolling over and over in gay abandon like a child in a field of green grass.

185

If any other bird lies on its back on the ground, it means just one thing; the bird is about to die. The first few times I found Jaffa on his back under the perches it frightened the life out of me. But I soon discovered he did it simply because he enjoyed it.

Even in the first few days I had Jaffa it became apparent that he was endowed less with intelligence than with bumbling good humour and persistence, rather like a bar-room bore. He wouldn't believe, and has never come to believe, the awful truth that Bluey and Blossom don't really like him. Each day while we were at the flat I used to let the three incredibly tattered-looking parrots out of their cages in the lounge for a couple of hours freedom. I would sit down on the settee to do some writing and keep an eye on them, and a line of parrots would start to wend its way across the carpet towards me. First came Bluey, confident and self-assured as always, walking slowly in that ponderous and exaggerated pigeon-toed fashion that parrots have, whistling half under his breath. A few feet behind him, slightly nervous, came Blossom, unsure of Bluey's bravado but equally unwilling to be left behind.

Behind her, scurrying on his much shorter legs, came Jaffa, chuckling and chattering with excitement. He never walked, but moved in short dashes, his legs flashing like pistons. Like all parrots, his feet turned in at an acute angle and running at this speed frequently resulted in one foot landing on top of the other and tripping him so that he went sprawling on his face with a cackle of alarm. He would sit up with a slightly dazed expression, shake his stubby feathers vigorously, and then dash off after Blossom again.

His eagerness would sometimes tempt him to try queue-hopping, or worse still to trample on Blossom's tail if there was no space to overtake. Blossom would spin round furiously, puffing out her feathers and swearing at him. Jaffa, as young as he was, always refused to retreat. He sat back on his tail and screamed as Blossom thrust her face in his, but still wouldn't take one pace backwards. Then would follow a few seconds of sharp fencing with their beaks before Blossom, with one final glare at him, set off again after Bluey. With no hesitation, Jaffa, his cheerful good humour immediately

186

restored, would scurry in her wake.

After several such incidents they would climb up the side of the settee and across my lap before climbing up my arm and to their favourite perching place on the back of the settee. Bluey came first, pausing affably in my lap to be stroked, followed by Blossom who sidled quickly past my hand. Then came Jaffa, who stayed long enough to grab a few of my papers and shout 'Yak-a-HOOO!' by way of greeting before scrambling after the other two parrots.

By the time Jaffa climbed to the back of the settee, Bluey and Blossom would be perched in cosy companionship, grooming each other's feathers. With no realisation that he was *de trop*, Jaffa galloped on his large feet to join them, pressing up close to Blossom's side.

There would be the inevitable altercation between them, Blossom puffed up, Jaffa sitting on his tail and screaming, and their beaks fencing briskly. Then Bluey and Blossom would move along several paces to escape his attentions, with Bluey always peering back with a slightly bewildered air, like an absent-minded father with too many children, saying: 'Er ... is he one of ours?' Jaffa had no discretion. He still has none. He just cannot believe that anyone or anything doesn't adore him and want his eager attentions twenty-four hours a day.

17

Florence and Dougal

SAKI MONKEY

It was impossible to give the Saki monkeys top priority with unpacking when the December consignment arrived. Because of its tender age and delicate constitution, the baby howler came first. The squirrel monkeys were unpacked next, as there were so many of them, and then the baby caiques and their parents. Then at last I was able to turn my attention to the Sakis.

I had suffered a great disappointment at the airport. Part of the invoice read: 'Three Sakis (one baby) in two crates.' But when I inspected the crates in great excitement, there was no baby. It had obviously died after the invoice had been made out and before the animals were dispatched; I wasn't surprised, but nevertheless it was a disappointment.

Ever since I had succeeded with the Old Man and his Missus, my greatest dream had been to achieve the same success with a baby Saki, something that had never been done in England. As far as we know, only one zoo in the world, Frankfurt, had been successful with a baby Saki; that one had thrived for nine months until it tragically died in an accident.

If only I could get hold of a baby Saki, I would throw all my heart into making it live; but the hope of obtaining one was forlorn.

When I came to uncrate the Sakis at home, I decided that they would have to share a fairly small cage just for the first night, until some of the other monkeys were collected and dispatched to their new homes. I wondered fleetingly whether their being sent in separate crates meant that they disagreed with each other, or whether it was careless extravagance on air freight costs by Mr Low.

I thought I'd cage the female first, as I wasn't at all happy about the appearance of the male and I wanted to give him a good inspection when I uncrated him. He was an old animal; his face, instead of being white, was yellow with age and his eyes were dull.

The female was very quiet and shy, but young and healthy-looking. I took the lid off her crate and held the open end of it against the cage, but she didn't move. I slipped my hand into the crate and gave her a gentle push towards the exit. She got up and very slowly walked out, going to the far side of the cage on the floor and turning to face me. It was so unlike the normal Saki bound I'd grown used to, that I paused a moment before closing the door, wondering if she was all right. I stared hard at her, but could see nothing wrong.

Then a tiny face, no bigger than a halfpenny, popped up out of the cape of long hair that curtained her chest: a naked and incredibly ugly face, with two sparkling eyes and enormous elfin ears. I stopped breathing for at least thirty seconds, not moving a muscle as I knelt there. I wanted to laugh and cry all at the same moment, but dared not move or make a sound for fear of frightening the mother. The tiny creature stared at me with frank interest. How could anything be so ugly and yet so beautiful, I thought, gazing in wonder at its skinny triangular face and outsize ears.

The female grew uneasy under my unblinking scrutiny. Putting her hand on top of the baby's head, she calmly but decisively pushed it down out of sight beneath her cape of fur.

I very carefully closed the door of the cage, crept out of the room, shut the door softly behind me and then bounded through the flat like a madman, shouting incoherently: 'I've got a baby! I've got a *baby Saki*!'

After my wild excitement had steadied a little, I went back into the animal-room. Obviously the mother and baby needed a better cage, the biggest and best in the place, and I preferred to move them straight away than to unsettle them with another move in a couple of days' time. It meant switching a lot of stock around and doubling them up, but at last the maternity ward was ready for them.

I gently pulled the Saki's present cage round until it joined doors with the new cage and the mother Saki needed little persuasion from me to walk through. As she climbed up to a thick perch, I had a good view of the baby spread-eagled on her chest. It was only four inches long from the top of its head to the base of its tail, a rather pathetic rat-like tail with no resemblance at all to the adult Sakis' bushy wonders. The body was dark, barely covered with short, sleek fur, not unlike a new-born puppy. Its legs and arms were long and very skinny, the tiny hands and feet clinging tightly to the mother's fur. The baby swivelled its head to look at me and gave a faint little trill like a small bird.

The female was very timid and unsettled. I sat on the floor and watched her for a while, trying to think myself into her mind to discover what it was that prevented her from relaxing. As I quietly watched, I became more and more convinced that there was something specific causing her tension.

I don't know what lucky thought led me to the right answer. I fetched one of the smallest crates, about eighteen inches square, and half-covered the open side of it, so that there was just a small entrance. I put an armful of straw inside it and put the box in a corner on the cage floor. I would have preferred to fix it up higher, but there was no way of doing this without a lot of hammering and noise. The chances of the monkey actually using the box were remote; small primates, like marmosets, titis and douroucoulis often use hollow trees as homes in the wild, but I knew of no species as large as a Saki with the same habit.

I had scarcely closed the cage door before the mother Saki climbed down from the perch and shambled through the narrow opening into the dark box. By crouching down low I could just see her contentedly arranging a bed out of the straw. Her attitude of extreme wariness had vanished. It was many weeks and dozens of zoological books later before I found a passing reference that said Sakis in the wild had sometimes been observed living in pairs in hollow trees.

I placed the water bowl and a dish of food within easy reach of the box, and soon a hand crept out and selected a grape. I covered the wire front of the cage with a sheet to give her the maximum of privacy, for only then, I thought, would she eat a proper meal. I was facing an extremely difficult decision. It was very possible that the mother's milk would dry up after the stress of travelling and a change of diet, and I probably wouldn't know for sure whether this had happened until I actually found the baby dead. There was also a chance that the female would abandon or even kill the baby.

Should I leave the baby with her, or remove it and try to rear it on a bottle? Even then, its chances of survival might be lowered instead of increased. I would have to carry it around with me all the time in order to be a proper substitute mother, and making up a suitable milk-feed would be sheer guesswork. I couldn't imagine that any zoo in the world had

191

ever made an analysis of Saki milk for butterfat, solids-not-fat and sugar content. Feeding with a wrongly-balanced mixture would result in an immediate digestive upset that almost certainly would kill the baby.

It was a terrible dilemma, especially as a baby Saki in this country was so rare as to be almost unheard of. None of them had ever survived more than a day or two, and quite apart from my own private feelings of intense interest, I felt a great responsibility to the zoological world as a whole to do the right thing for this baby. Professional zoologists are not impressed by inept meddling from amateurs, although none of the ones I've met have ever been patronising towards me. But if I lost this baby Saki through some elementary error, I felt I would never be able to hold my head up again.

Eventually I decided to leave the baby with its mother. I had to take a gamble on her not abandoning or killing it during the first night, and after that I hoped that if her milk did in fact dry up the baby would start wailing with hunger so that I was warned in time to try bottle-feeding.

After settling the mother and baby, I turned my attention to the male Saki. I removed the top of his crate, put on a leather glove and reached in to him. He blinked at me out of dull eyes and made no attempt to move away. Something, I felt, was terribly wrong. I pulled off the glove and picked him up. There was no resistance from him, none of the natural agitation I expected.

I laid him in my lap and ran my hands over him to see if perhaps he had a broken limb or festering sore to cause the fever he was obviously suffering. As I felt his backbone and then his ribs, I felt a shock of horror jolt through me. He was like an inmate of Belsen, nothing more than a skeleton beneath his heavy coat of long hair.

'What have they done to you?' I whispered. But I had already guessed. This Saki had been psychologically unable to accept captivity, and when caught by the local villagers had simply refused to eat. Instead of releasing him again, as any-one with any humanity would have done, they had gambled on the monkey's long shaggy coat hiding the evidence of self-inflicted starvation and had sold him to Mr Low, who had innocently sent the monkey on to me almost immediately.

192

His thin body was cold and seemed to have no weight to it. I held him close to me, trying to warm him. I tried feeding him some sugar and water, adding a few drops of Abidec, but it wouldn't stay down for more than a few moments. He did a little better with plain warmed water, keeping down a couple of spoonfuls, but apart from helping to quench his thirst it did him little good. I knew I couldn't save him; the most I could do was to make sure he didn't die alone.

The old Saki lay cradled in my arms like a sick child, his eyes fastened on my face.

At midnight I dimmed the lights and the other animals settled to a contented and rustling sleep. Outside the storm raged, tossing the big fir trees and rattling the windows. The old Saki died peacefully just before two o'clock, his hand resting in mine, his first and final gesture of friendship.

I stayed where I was for a while, holding his lifeless body against me, my throat aching. I felt a great burden of guilt. But there was nothing an importer could do to prevent something of this particular nature from happening—except give up importing. I was very close to that decision when I heard a slight noise behind me. I twisted my head and looked through a gap in the curtain over the front of the female Saki's cage. She had come out of the box and was taking a long drink of water. She moved on to the other dish and started sorting over the food. She finished the grapes, cautiously tried a piece of Cheddar cheese and found it to her liking, and then started on the banana. The baby clung to her chest, swivelling its head like an owl in order to see everything. It seemed impossible that such a tiny and delicate creature could possibly survive importation. And yet it had already come through the hardest part, a journey of several thousand miles to a country where the climatic temperature was 40° cooler. If I did everything right, I thought, there must be a chance—perhaps a good chance—of the baby pulling through.

I looked down again at the old dead Saki in my arms, almost certainly the baby's father. I couldn't give up, I could see that now. For as long as there were new facts to learn about animals that may one day be threatened in the wild state, then I wanted to be one of the people contributing to this knowledge, in however small a way. I wasn't a trained zoologist, but I had discovered a certain knack with delicate primates and perhaps this was where I could break new areas of ground. I had already succeeded with adult Sakis, so I was among the handful of people who theoretically stood a chance of success with a baby Saki.

I went to bed for a few hours, but was back in the animal-room early in the morning. As I pulled back the curtain on the cage, I was half expecting to find the cold, limp body of the baby on the floor. But there was no sign of it, and the dish of food was half-eaten. I got down and peered into the box and the female stared back at me passively. I couldn't see the baby. I spoke to the mother softly and at the sound of my voice an ugly little head popped out of her cape of fur to investigate. I started breathing again. The first crucial night had been survived. I gave the female a handful of mealworms and she stuffed their wriggling bodies into her mouth appreciatively.

The baby survived the second night, too. The mother showed no signs of abandoning it, and I felt this danger had passed. As the baby was quiet and seemed contented, the mother's milk had apparently not dried up. By the third day I was in a fever to know the sex of the baby; if it was a male I was quite determined that it would become a permanent member of the family, but if it was a female its naturally timid nature would debar it from ever becoming really tame.

My excuse for a brief inspection of the baby came because the female was a bad housekeeper and had strewn the sleeping box with dropped food. I carefully pulled the box to the door of the cage and removed the soiled straw and debris by hand. The female sat watching me cautiously, with her back against the side of the crate and the baby in clear view spread-eagled on her chest. I moved my hand nearer, very slowly and cautiously, talking softly to her without pause. She still didn't object when at last my hand touched the baby's tail, moving it just fractionally. It was a boy. His head swivelled to watch me, and his pink toothless gums showed as he trilled at me.

I named him the same day. I had seen the Magic Round-about on television, and for the first time it occurred to me that both Dougal and Florence had a strong facial resemblance to Saki monkeys. So mother and son were christened Florence and Dougal, the magic Sakis.

194

Another night passed, a second and third, we reached the end of the first week and Dougal was still alive. Florence was a poor feeder compared to the Old Man and his Missus, and I had to spend hours trying to persuade her to try new foods apart from her favourite grapes, bananas and mealworms. I offered hard-boiled egg, lettuce, raw steak, nuts, sunflower seed, bread, sweet biscuit, apples, raisins, dates, oranges, carrots, cucumber, honey, Kellogg's Cornflakes, melon and porridge oats. She firmly refused all milk, Farex and Complan, but I struck lucky with Lactol dog biscuits and she would usually eat one with each meal. She also ate one or two pieces of cheese each day, either cream cheese or Cheddar. As with all the animals, Abidec drops played a big part in her diet, not only to keep her healthy but also in passing the vitamins on to Dougal through her milk.

Before the animals arrived in December, I had already arranged to go away for one night at Christmas, and Adrian, who lived only a mile away, had agreed to come and give the stock the three necessary feeds during my absence. When I realised I had a baby Saki on my hands, it looked for a while as if we would have to cancel our arrangements, but Dougal was thriving so well at the end of the intervening nine days that I decided to go away after all. I felt confident in leaving the Sakis' welfare in Adrian's hands, as he'd had a fair measure of experience with general stock.

Needless to say, I still quietly worried about the Sakis during my two days' holiday, even though I could be reached by telephone if there was any emergency. Health-wise, too, I was feeling under the weather; what had threatened as a bad cold at Heathrow Airport had developed into a severe cough.

When I returned on Boxing Day I was glad to find all well with the animals. The Sakis seemed contented, and the baby's head popped up to regard me with lively interest.

During a coughing bout that night I was woken by a sharp jab of pain in my chest. It didn't go away and hurt if I moved or breathed deeply. I was sure I'd cracked a rib. My doctor prodded and poked it the next day, said there was no sign of a fracture and gave me a prescription for some cough linctus. Coughing was extremely painful during the next few days, as was bending down to clean out the cages and feed the animals.

But then the pain eased and my cough went away.

Three days later the cough returned worse than before. Several times each day I would have uncontrollable bouts lasting five or ten minutes when I could do nothing but struggle to get my breath. One such spasm of coughing took place in the animal-room when I was preparing the afternoon feed, and I leaned against the wall with my eyes watering. I gasped as a pain sliced through my lower ribs; this time I felt the bones grate together.

The doctor agreed to send me along to the local hospital for an X-ray, and also for a blood-test in case I had contracted any tropical disease while I was in Guyana, although it was already two months since my return to England.

I hadn't heard the result of either test when I had to travel up to London for the day at the end of the first week in January. First I spent a couple of hours in the *Sunday Times* offices, checking the proofs of an article I had helped to write about the Guyana Ranchers' rebellion which had taken place a few days before.

From there I travelled to Halpern's shop in North London to deliver some birds. He had just received a tame four-year-old chimpanzee, and I found myself inveigled into baby-sitting with her for a couple of hours to keep her out of mischief while Halpern finished his work.

I didn't really mind, as she was a delightful and hilariously funny creature. She used a child's potty for its proper purpose, was adept at picking up the telephone receiver and dialling a number at random, and was very partial to a mug of tea. She was also a heavy smoker and each time I lit up she screamed furiously if I didn't light one for her as well. It was no idle trick, either; she really enjoyed smoking, inhaling deeply and then blowing lazy smoke rings as she lay on her back with one arm under her head and one foot casually hitched on the other knee. She was so well-trained that she wouldn't drop a lighted cigarette end on the floor but would wander around until she found an ashtray in which to stub it out.

But she was also a rough playmate and I took several playful punches on my already painful ribs. At one time she took a flying leap into my arms. She was no lightweight and the impact against my chest made me feel dizzy for a moment.

The chimp meant me no harm in her boisterous play, but my ribs took a pounding from her and by the time I caught the coach back to Cobham I was feeling very shaky.

The following day I telephoned my doctor for the result of the tests. Both were negative, the X-ray showing no evidence of any fractures and the blood-test revealing no organic disease.

'Then what *is* wrong with me?' I asked.

'You've just been working too hard. You know you have, particularly these last few months.'

A black cloud of depression settled on me as I put down the receiver. Was I suddenly becoming a hypochondriac? Were the cough, the pain in my ribs and the feeling of apathy no more than stress symptoms brought on by living too hectic a life? I felt sure there must be some other reason. During the next few days the cough cleared up and the pain in my ribs eased. Maybe, I thought doubtfully, the doctor was right after all.

Through Adrian I had some news of Brian, who I hadn't seen since the end of November. He was still ill and not responding to treatment. His doctors now suspected tuberculosis and were thinking of admitting him to hospital for tests. I had a sudden thought.

'Has he got a cough?' I asked Adrian.

'No, just a wildly fluctuating temperature. He looked pretty ill when I saw him.'

It was the only time that I considered the possibility of our illnesses being connected, but I immediately dismissed the idea from my mind as our symptoms were totally different; he didn't have a cough, and I didn't have a temperature.

A couple of weeks passed with me feeling no more discomfort than unusual tiredness and irritability. But then the cough flared up again, even worse than before. During one of the paroxysms two more of my ribs fractured simultaneously. I still know of no more painful combination than cracked ribs and an uncontrollable cough. The fear of sneezing actually haunted me.

I insisted on having another X-ray at the hospital; either I had fractured ribs, or I was going round the bend. The radiologist remembered me from my first visit, and in conversation it materialised that she had had no instructions to look for rib fractures last time, and these would very likely not show up on a general X-ray.

As I was incapable of either straightening up or leaning back under my own power, she called in a doctor and together they managed to lay me flat on a table, where they took close-up pictures of the four areas of pain that I indicated. The four fractures were clearly revealed on the X-ray plates. At least, I thought with relief, I have proof that my mind isn't going. The case was referred back to my own doctor. It was the greatest anti-climax when he did no more than write out a prescription for some pain-killing pills.

'Aren't you going to strap the ribs or something?' I asked almost desperately.

'That often does more harm than good.'

'But if the cough doesn't go away I could go on cracking more ribs!'

He wrote out a prescription for a different cough linctus.

'But the main thing is for you to ease up on the work,' he advised.

He reminded me that I'd been galloping around South America, with all the organisation and the welfare of a good number of people as a responsibility, that I'd travelled something like twenty thousand miles that year, organising tours and collecting animals, and that instead of resting when I came back I had started writing a book, and was dealing with a great many animals. There was no doubt that he meant it kindly, that the diagnosis made sense to him. I have wondered several times since whether he ever got to hear how wrong he'd been.

As one last safeguard against the possibility of my having an organic disease he sent me to the hospital for another blood-test. It was negative. It was bound to be. The virus that was infecting me would be undetected during a normal blood-test. The virus could only be revealed by a specific and unusual laboratory test. If my illness had flared out of the chronic stage into the acute stage at that particular time, I don't doubt that I would have died for lack of an accurate diagnosis. There was to be another couple of months of bliss-ful ignorance before a lucky chance saved not only me but several other people at the very last moment.

198

18

Dougal's Progress

Although the weeks that followed Christmas were over-shadowed by an uneasy acceptance of mild but persistent ill-health, through them ran the thread of joy my animals gave me. Betsy, the baby baboon, and Jenny, the grivet, were still with me and had wriggled so deep into my affections that I wondered if I would ever be able to part with them.

The baby capuchin was also still there, but the two adult female capuchins had been sold, and Sarah, the pig-tailed monkey, had gone to Weston Zoo. There were nearly always a variety of birds around the place: quail, conures, a succession of African Greys, and the two brown-shouldered parrots from Zambia which nobody seemed interested in buying, although they were attractive-looking birds.

Bluey, Blossom and Jaffa were all doing well. And Florence and Dougal thrived. I spent many hours in the animal-room each day. The baby Saki grew and developed amazingly quickly. At the end of four weeks he measured six inches from head to base of tail, a growth of two inches since his arrival. He now began to make short exploratory trips away from his mother's protection, investigating the wood shavings in the bottom of the cage and the dish of food that as yet was only a plaything to him.

He was constantly curious and interested in everything around him. He was quite unafraid of me and although he couldn't be tempted to stray far from his mother, he would come to the entrance of the sleeping box and put his friendly little paw into my hand. His white face fur was beginning to grow and he was already far less ugly than on his arrival. The black fur over the rest of his body had lengthened consider-ably, and his tail had fluffed out with a quarter-of-an-inch growth of silky hair.

Florence remained very reserved, although she soon learned to accept food from my hand. She was always the picture of passivity, but although she tolerated my friendly overtures to her son for a reasonable length of time, sooner or later she would quietly put an end to it by picking him up and thrusting him under her cape of hair, like a Victorian matron tucking a letter into her bosom for safe-keeping. Dougal wasn't always ready to accept maternal discipline in this way, but as soon as his head popped up through her thick mantle of fur the palm of Florence's hand would firmly push him down again.

He was still inclined to topple on to his face when he tried to walk, but he was progressing in other ways. He now often rode jockey-style on Florence's back when she came out of the box, instead of clinging to her chest as previously. He became increasingly venturesome when his mother was up on the perches, climbing down from her back and wobbling along the perch as if it was a tightrope.

Florence seemed to take little notice of him on these occasions, but as soon as he fell off the perch—which he always did sooner or later—she would quite casually reach out a hand and catch him in mid-air, grabbing his leg, an arm, or even his tail. Unflustered by her son's narrow escape, she would hold him to her chest until his spidery, flailing limbs caught hold of her fur.

Their sleeping arrangements provided Dougal with a degree of comfort worthy of the Ritz. Sitting in the box, surrounded by a thick bed of straw, Florence would place the baby between her feet so that his head rested on her stomach. Then, using her hands, she would carefully arrange her great bushy tail over him like a thick eiderdown. Finally she curled in a loose ball, head down, so that the arch of her body completely closed him in.

I should have imagined Dougal to be unable even to stir beneath all this, but whenever I unintentionally disturbed them while they were asleep, Dougal's investigating head would pop out of the sea of Florence's fur like a ping-pong ball bobbing to the surface of a lake, a white face with two sparkling eyes, bat-ears and a shiny black nose. Curiously enough, and to my disappointment, I never once witnessed the baby suckling from Florence. This, apparently, could only be performed during the most private and secluded moments.

It was at the end of the first month that I allowed Dougal to be photographed for the first time. Until then I had struggled with the predicament of allowing the disturbance of photography and risking the possibility of Florence abandoning the baby as a result; or not photographing them and accepting the strong likelihood that Dougal would die anyway during this time, leaving us with no photographic record. As photographs of baby Sakis were, to say the least, rare, they would be of world-wide zoological interest.

It was a hard decision, but I held out against Adrian's pleas for the first four weeks. By then the real danger period was past, the mother seemed well settled and the baby grew more lively every day. Photographing them wasn't easy, for we had to take great care not to upset them. When my cough wasn't being troublesome I helped Adrian by holding the screens to prevent them moving away from the camera, and by feeding Florence with tit-bits to keep her interested. She regarded the camera with the greatest suspicion, but we were always so quiet and slow-moving that she never became really upset. Time was of no importance during these sessions, patience meant everything.

Florence was persistently obstructive. After lying on the floor on our stomachs for perhaps half-an-hour, with the camera set ready and focussed, our cramped limbs complaining creakily, we should be rewarded by Florence moving sufficiently to reveal a perfect picture of Dougal. And then, before Adrian had time to release the shutter, Florence would sabotage it by placing her hand over the baby or turning round so that her back was to the lens. And then we should have to start all over again. At last, after several weeks, we had the set of photographs we required, and a pair of bent backs we could have done without.

Dougal loved to chew my finger, and because of this I knew immediately when he cut his first tooth six weeks after his arrival, no more than a tiny transparent pin in his pink gum. Several others erupted during the next few days, and about the same time he started putting things in his mouth, not chewing so much as trying them out for taste; woodshavings, straw, Florence's tail, the metal edge of the water-tin, small pieces of food—he was quite indiscriminate in his experiments. After another two weeks he began to nibble at food, first a tiny piece of apple, then next day a halved grape, then banana and sweet biscuit. Within a short time he was eating small but regular amounts of hard food in addition to his mother's milk.

When Dougal was six weeks old I fixed a narrow perch

inside the sleeping-box so that he could practise in safety the acrobatics that looked so dangerous when his mother took him outside on the high perches. Dougal was delighted and spent much of each day swinging, climbing and walking along it with his jerky juvenile movements. The perch was also a good teething-ring and soon bore evidence of his strengthening teeth.

At the end of two months he measured another two inches in length, eight in all from head to base of tail. The growth pattern indicated a gain of half-an-inch a week, and in retrospect I would place him at no more than one week old when he arrived in England. His face was now as large as a half-crown, compared to a halfpenny on arrival.

At two months he was very well-covered with fur and the cape over his shoulders was already over one-and-a-half inches long. His face was now completely white and he was recognisable for what he was, a male white-faced Saki, but his enormous ears were still much in evidence. Adult Sakis discreetly hide their large ears beneath a shaggy head of hair.

I spent many happy hours just sitting and watching Dougal play. He was one of nature's tiny miracles, and I felt almost maternally protective towards him.

At the beginning of February I fractured two more ribs from coughing, making a total of six. This time I didn't bother to tell my doctor, as I still had a supply of cough linctus and pain-killers, neither of which seemed to do me much good. But the pain was really bad this time, and I had little sleep at nights. By the end of the week I felt exhausted and on the verge of cracking up; I felt positive there was something radically wrong with me, but knew I would never be able to convince the doctor.

By the weekend I was in such a wretched state that I telephoned the doctor and asked him to call. When he arrived he hid his irritation under a polite but firm exterior. He didn't rush away again immediately, as he might have done. He spent twenty minutes trying to talk some stern but kind sense into me. Two blood-tests had proved negative, absolute proof, he said, that nothing was organically wrong with me. I had to accept that it was all in my mind and pull myself together.

He made out a prescription for some tranquillisers which

I had no intention of taking and glanced round at the five parrots in the lounge, Bluey, Blossom, Jaffa and two African grey 'growlers' I was trying to tame. I had to cut down on all this work, he advised, give it up, take a holiday, stop worrying.

'It's me, not my mind, that's sick,' I objected, but I knew it was no use trying to convince him. His patience wore thin at my stubbornness and he soon left. I never saw him again after that, so he didn't really have a chance to correct his diagnosis.

During the following week my cough once more vanished and I began to feel considerably better. The fluctuating course of my illness was the main reason why I didn't seek medical advice elsewhere, apart from the fact that I liked my own doctor. Each time my discomfort was on the point of driving me to see another doctor, the symptoms would clear up again.

I spoke to Brian on the telephone a couple of times, but although he seemed to be making a steady if slow recovery— with his doctors admitting their bafflement after tuberculosis was disproved—he was still not well enough to come down and see the baby Saki.

I myself began to feel so much better that I started to pay proper attention to the many enquiries for stock from various zoos. I had already decided back in December that I wanted to start an importing business on a much larger scale if I could find suitable premises. After looking at several places I saw a small house not far from the airport, with a fifty-foot long outhouse and a paddock. It would be ideal for my purpose, although I would have to wait several weeks before I could have possession.

With these plans so near the hatching stage, I was reluctant to turn away enquiries for stock, as I needed the goodwill of these zoos for the future. So I decided to import a small consignment just to keep things ticking over, from an exporter I'd heard about in Thailand.

The animals arrived one evening in the middle of February after a flight that had been much delayed by fog and snow. At one point it looked as if the KLM flight would end up in Spain, and I began to get really worried for there were a pair of delicate spectacled langurs in the consignment which needed a very specialised diet. I never fail to be impressed by the helpfulness of the airlines I have dealt with when importing animals—BOAC, KLM and Air Lingus. The trouble and interest they have taken has been exceptional. When animals are *en route,* telexes between the countries involved fly back and forth without regard for expense, and on occasions where flights are delayed or having a rough passage the freight offices at Heathrow make a point of keeping the importer notified of each change of situation.

Luckily for my Thai animals, there was a brief lifting in the cloud at Amsterdam in the late afternoon and the Bangkok flight was able to put down safely. The next telephone call from the Heathrow office told me that the fog had closed down again at Amsterdam, so my animals would be kept there for the night and would leave on the first London flight tomorrow.

By then it was past six o'clock, so I reduced the heat in the animal-room, dimmed the lights and started to cook my supper. I knew the consignment would be well taken care of at Amsterdam, which has probably the finest animal hostel in the world. But at eight-thirty that evening there was another call from Heathrow. The fog at Amsterdam had lifted again. My animals had been put on board the London flight and were due to arrive at any moment.

I turned up the heat and lighting in the animal-room, and made a mad dash for the airport. The uncertainty and tension accompanying importing livestock is enough to shred your nerves to pieces!

Some of the stock I ordered hadn't been included in the consignment: the white squirrels, pygmy owlets and fairy bluebirds. But the rest were there: the parakeets, slow lorises, rainbow water snakes, tree shrews and two spectacled langurs. As I gazed into the langurs' crate, I found my heart captured as it had been on my first meeting with Saki monkeys. I had never met spectacled langurs before and I was immediately enchanted with not only their beauty but also their languid grace and exceptionally gentle natures.

Their coats were long and silky, a dark, dusky-grey in colour, and they had long slender tails. Their hands and feet were also long and slim, almost artistic-looking, and the large white rings around their eyes and mouths made me think at once of the Black and White Minstrels. Their most striking

205

feature, however, was their eyes, large and round and liquid, having that particular glow of tenderness with which a mother regards her new-born baby. Their movements were graceful and unhurried and they showed no fear at all of me, holding my hand and accepting pieces of banana with regal good manners. Since that moment I have always had an ambition to own a breeding colony of spectacled langurs; perhaps one day I shall be lucky.

Sexing the three slow lorises was an extraordinarily difficult task. Their external anatomy seemcd to be identical and after I watched them climbing around their pen for a while, with their ultra-slow and jerky mode of locomotion, I began to suspect that, male or female, I had three of the same sex instead of the two females and one male I required.

A manual examination seemed called for, and I'm glad to say that I was sensible enough to put on leather gloves first, even though the animals were so placid-looking. Slow lorises, although they are smaller than a cat and almost sloth-like in their speed, must rate as one of the most difficult species to handle, at least until you learn all their little tricks. For one thing they have almost no neck, and it's difficult to get a good grip on them. But the main problem lies in the fantastic gripping power of their curiously square hands. Try to pluck a slow loris off a branch or perch and you'll be all day on the job, unless the wood happens to break in two.

After a couple such abortive attempts to take the loris of my choice out of the cage, I began to appreciate what I was up against. So I cunningly waited until the animal started climbing about again and had both front feet off the perch before I reached in and took it firmly around the neck with one gloved hand, while with my other hand I started gently peeling its toes one by one off the perch.

It wasn't a bad idea really, except that by the time I had detached both back feet the creature's slowly flailing arms at the other end had made contact with the wire side of the cage. I patiently began to peel its fingers off one at a time, but before I had finished the task the loris's body arched round and both back feet took a firm grip on the wire. To add insult to injury, or *vice versa,* the loris chose that moment to twist its head and bite my finger hard. Its expression was completely passive and unflustered as it did so, unlike my own.

I temporarily retired, well and truly defeated by the tiny creature. But the sexing had to be done and after a short rest I returned to the slow-motion affray. This time I persuaded each loris to climb on to a broomstick which I then took out of the cage before I picked them up. Some time and several bitten fingers later I established that the lorises were the required two females and one male, the only discernible difference being a hidden vent in the females.

When I was examining one of the females I noticed very slight signs, no more than a faint solidity about her abdomen, that she might be pregnant. She was the one destined for Paignton Zoo, along with the langurs, and I mentioned the possibility of pregnancy to their Superintendent when he telephoned me later in the day.

I was delighted to have my tentative prediction confirmed almost immediately, for when I went into the animal-room early next morning there was a new-born baby loris clinging to the female's back. The rather sleepy-looking creature was only three inches long, but fully-furred and an almost perfect replica of an adult loris except in size. I have no idea whether slow lorises born in captivity are a rare or common occurrence, but at the time I was so wrapped up with the miracle of Florence and Dougal that the birth of the baby loris was no more to me than a pleasant but fairly unimportant incident.

In any case I am not particularly inspired by slow lorises, or the very similar African pottos. Although their large round eyes and teddy-bear look makes them attractive, I have found nothing in their temperament other than an exasperating mixture of stupidity and stubbornness, and the daytime view of them is seldom more than a completely round ball of brown fur clinging to the perch. But it's a personal view; probably someone somewhere loves lorises as I love Sakis.

19

End of an Era and a New Start

TAMANDUA ANTEATER

Ill-luck seldom comes in single doses; frequently it triggers off a succession of related and unrelated events that can mount into something of a tidal wave.

The escalade of events in March and April 1969 started off innocuously enough with my discovering soon after the Thailand consignment that I could obtain no extension of my lease of the flat. There was little time for all the arrangements I had to make—not only finding temporary accommodation for myself and storing the furniture, but also for dispersing all the animals with me at the time. It looked as if there would be an interval of about three weeks between my moving out of the flat and then into the new house.

With so little time at my disposal, I had to rent an expensive furnished house at Willesden in North London.

During those last frantically busy days at the flat when I was sorting and packing my many possessions to take with me or be stored, and arranging temporary and permanent homes for all the animals, I was thankful that my health seemed so much improved. I had no idea it was the lull before the storm.

I sent the last of the orders off to various zoos and was finally left with a reasonably small collection of animals to farm out in one way or another. A Mr and Mrs Chesham, who owned a pet-shop near Portsmouth and who had often visited me to buy squirrel monkeys, proved the greatest help at this time. They agreed to take the majority of my animals on a sale-or-return basis until I was established in the new premises in Surrey. Three days before we moved Mr Chesham came over with his van to collect Betsy, Jenny, the baby capuchin, the pair of brown-shouldered parrots, an Amazon parrot, and a mixed collection of parakeets, Pekin robins and other small birds. He agreed that he wouldn't sell Betsy or Jenny without consulting me first, as they had to have special homes, but thought that in any case they would be an attraction for his shop. The Cheshams were an obliging and friendly couple, and I've never ceased to regret that I unknowingly handed over what amounted to a time-bomb to them.

Bluey, Blossom and Pinto would come to the rented house with me, Adrian would look after Jaffa, and Janine was able to board my two cats. It's only in writing it down that I realise the procession of animals out of that flat must have resembled the disembarkation of Noah's Ark. It never actually *seemed* crowded, though.

I was left with the heart-searching problem of what to do with Florence and Dougal. Monkeys in the spare room would obviously not be allowed by my new landlord, and as he lived right next door there was not much chance of smuggling them in. Only a wildlife-minded person could have understood the vital necessity of my keeping the monkeys with me so that the baby's welfare wasn't threatened.

I really had two choices. Either I could ask Ken Smith to look after them for me for a few weeks, which I knew he'd be delighted to do, or I could agree to Adrian, who had just taken a room in London, having them with him. If Ken's Zoo had been nearer, I would have had no hesitation in sending them there. But it was nearly two hundred miles away and the weather was bitter. Apart from everything else, if my plans worked out, the Sakis would also have to make the long journey back again at the end of the month.

At last I decided against it, feeling that it would be much better for the monkeys simply to be moved into a slightly smaller cage and taken by hired van the twenty miles to Adrian's room in Camden Town.

I delivered them to Adrian on the morning of the first Sunday in March, and I moved out of the flat the same evening. Dougal had been with me for exactly eleven weeks. He now measured nine inches from the top of his head to the base of his tail, his hair had reached almost shaggy proportions and he was full of vitality and mischief. As I said goodbye to them, I cursed the luck that was temporarily separating us at such an interesting stage of his development. I had tried my hardest not to become too attached to the baby, for all along his chances of survival had been slim and I didn't want to break my heart if he died. But it was no use; I'd gone hook, line and sinker overboard for Dougal.

The first few days at Willesden seemed strange with so little to do. I supposed doubtfully that it was a pleasant rest, but I missed all the animals badly and hardly knew what to do with myself. My mother and her sister Dolores came to lunch with me the following Sunday. It was a fateful day, but it started off peacefully enough, although early in the morning I felt a bit peculiar, not at all unwell but light-headed, as if I was rather intoxicated. The feeling persisted through lunch, pleasant chatter with my mother and aunt, and through tea in the late afternoon. But then my skin began to tingle and I felt shivery.

Just after tea, Adrian arrived. The news he brought with him brought my little world crashing down around my ears.

Dougal was dead.

I didn't let the tears come until the house was empty and silent, when Adrian had left, and my mother and aunt had gone to the station. And then I cried as if I had lost my own baby.

That night I became seriously ill for the first time in my life. I lay in bed for several days with a soaring temperature, only hazily aware of my surroundings. With the effects of the fever and another bout of pleurisy, plus yet two more fractured ribs, I was too muddled in my mind to wonder if I had more than a bad attack of influenza aggravated by my distress at Dougal's death. Naturally I hadn't blamed Adrian in any way. He'd given the monkeys the best of care, but on the fifth day he had found the baby dead underneath the perches showing no outward cause and having displayed no prior symptoms. It was only later—when it was also too late to save Florence from dying—that we realised the monkeys had almost certainly died from the same virus that was infecting me, now in its dangerous final stage.

Once in hospital, however, exhaustive tests having proved negative, a young doctor had an inspiration and asked whether I'd had any contact with parrots. When I told him I was a zoological importer, handling many dozens of parrots in the previous six months, everything suddenly fell into place as easily as the last few pieces of a jig-saw puzzle. I had psittacosis, a killing virus transmitted to humans by infected parrot-like birds. This was the first proved case of psittacosis in that particular hospital's history, although since then there have been a number of further separate outbreaks caused by newly-imported parrots.

With the hospital, the Ministries of Health and Agriculture, and myself all co-operating, we managed to trace all contacts with the parrot-like birds I'd had in my possession since my return from South America. Blood-tests (specifically for psittacosis) discovered five more infected people. Symptoms ranged from massive pneumonia and scepticaemia to a mild sore throat. Eradication of the virus from our systems, once the vital diagnosis had been made, was quick and simple; just one week's course of terramycin. The after-effects, however, mainly weakness and lack of stamina, affected several of us for a few months afterwards.

The culprits were quickly found by a process of elimination, not even birds I myself had imported but the two brown-shouldered parrots from Zambia which had been with me for several months without showing any sign of disease. Faced at first with the possibility of having to destroy Jaffa, Bluey and Blossom in case they were affected with the virus, I discovered from veterinary authorities that a two-week course of terramycin would make them 'safe'. Since then I have made a point of giving a terramycin course to all the parrot-like birds I import.

Once again my life veered off its planned course. My long illness meant I lost the chance of having the house I wanted for continuing my importing. Too weak at first to work, and now very short of money. Janine took me under her wing and in a remarkable show of friendship opened her house not only to me but also the remainder of my varied animals. Slowly recovering, I had to start thinking about getting a job to support myself. The zoological world now seemed a closed door to me, for without capital I could no longer import animals. Just as I was on the point of accepting an agricultural job, Ken and Trudy Smith heard of my predicament and offered me a job in one of their children's zoos in the West Country for the summer season.

And that's how I 'discovered' Shaldon, the tiny and picturesque fishing village on the South Devon coast which has become my much-loved home. Flanking one side of Teignmouth harbour, where a fleet of sailing dinghies lie moored, Shaldon is a colourful jumble of small cottages with a confusing maze of narrow alleyways between them. 'Shaldon wasn't planned,' as someone once said, 'it just happened.' From the long bridge spanning the harbour, the main street winds through the little village, leads alongside the beach and then begins to mount the steep cliff called the Ness that dominates the entrance to the harbour, its rugged red face topped with a thatch of green woods. It is here, on top of the Ness, that the tiny children's zoo is situated which I managed for Ken for two seasons, just above the old smuggler's tunnel whose long flights of damp steps lead down to Ness Cove.

Although so small, the zoo is well-fitted with pens and holds a surprising variety of animals: three or four monkeys, genets, civets, hornbills, squirrels, owls, hawks, mongooses, parrots, cockatoos, a large selection of small birds, a lamb, a kid, small rodents and countless rabbits and guinea-pigs.

Minnie, a banded mongoose from Africa, was one of my particular favourites. She had been someone's pet in Nigeria and when she arrived in this country she came straight to me at Shaldon. Described by her previous owner as 'hand-tame', Trudy nevertheless warned me on the telephone to be cautious with her. Trudy doesn't fully trust any mongoose, being convinced that sooner or later they will all bite the hand that feeds them. By the second day I had decided that Minnie was truly tame and a most delightful creature. She was never still, constantly bounding, climbing, turning somersaults and tearing everything to pieces. She could get hours of play out of the smallest things, a stick of wood, a snail, a ball or a small rotting log.

A cardboard box was one of her favourite toys, although one seldom lasted more than half-an-hour before being demolished. With one blow of her paw she would turn it upside down, then with a flick of her long nose she would lift the edge just enough for her fat body to slide inside. Visitors would then be treated to the astonishing sight of a seemingly-animated box rushing round the pen at breakneck speed. Not even her feet showed below the rim. Now and then she would stop and poke her nose out to make sure she still had an appreciative audience, then with a snort of excitement she would charge off once more with the box completely covering her. Eventually tiring of this, she would worry the cardboard base until she had made a 'back entrance' and, turning the box on its side, she would start a mad-cap circuit of her cage in a mongoose-obstacle-race, alternating leaping over the box with leaping through it—like a lion through a hoop, until, completely out of breath, she flopped on top of the box and squashed it beyond further use. Panting and wriggling her fat body, she would grin at me, obviously asking for another box.

Minnie adored having her back scratched. When I held her in my arms she would push her nose under my chin, stretch her arms and legs out full-length, and close her eyes in near-ecstasy as I scratched her bristly back. Visitors were also expected to co-operate, and they soon realised what she wanted when she sat with her back pressed against the wire, throwing glances over her shoulder at them and making encouraging little snuffles and squeaks. But the second they stopped a sometimes lengthy session of obligingly scratching her back, she would erupt into passionate pleading for them to start again.

Trudy remained unconvinced, sure in her own mind that Minnie would turn on me one day. It happened after about two months. I always had the mongoose running loose around the zoo early in the morning when I was cleaning out all the pens and collecting dishes. One morning Minnie discovered a piece of stale meat in the waste bucket and grabbed it in her mouth. Not wanting her to eat stale food, I spoke sharply to her. She backed away from me, still holding on to the meat, and emitted a high-pitched chukking cry. In future I recognised and respected that cry as a signal that she would attack if I didn't retire immediately, but now, not realising the significance of the new voice, I reached forward and pulled the meat from her mouth. Of course, to put it plainly, it was a damned stupid thing to do, and I paid for it. As I straightened up, Minnie exploded with anger, leapt two feet into the air and buried her teeth in my thumb. She remained dangling in mid-air, her jaws clamped to my hand and my blood spilling down over her. Her bite was so powerful for such a small creature that she almost took my thumb right off.

Managing to shake off her firm grip at last, I wrapped a cloth around my hand while I considered how best to get an angry mongoose back in its pen before I had to open the zoo door for the first visitors. But to my surprise, after about half-a-minute to think things over, Minnie came back to apologise for her unfriendly behaviour. As I picked her up (I admit, with some initial misgivings) she licked my face and rubbed her head against my cheek in a confusion of shame. Trudy, of course, said 'I told you so' when she heard about the incident, but, as I pointed out, we could hardly blame Minnie for attacking me when I did such a stupid thing. She has remained very tame over the last two years, although still very possessive over her food. This led her to take another small chunk out of my hand a while later, but I still think she's one of the most delightful animals I have ever known.

There were other animal characters for which I had a great affection. Gladys, a pied hornbill who loved to have her throat rubbed, during which she would slowly bend her head and neck back in the most extraordinary contortions. And Tuki, a toco toucan who was so tame that I could trust him to take a grape from between my lips with his large brilliantly-coloured beak. Tocos, are a most attractive species, with gleaming black-and-white bodies, rather like a penguin's colouration, and flamboyant orange and yellow beaks. Tuki was inordinantly proud of his beak, and when I put his daily bath into the pen he would perch on the side of the pan dipping his big beak into the water and thoroughly scrubbing it with first one claw and then the other, with the high-speed motion of someone brushing his teeth. After a good twenty or thirty minutes concentrated effort cleaning his beak, Tuki thought the rest of him needed scant attention; nothing more than a split-second plunge into the water.

Not such a favourite of mine, however, was Henry, a giant hornbill about the size of a vulture, with big feet, long, curly film-star eyelashes and a really massive curved beak. Although I didn't like to admit it, I was just a tiny bit nervous of Henry, and Henry knew it. He had a diabolical sense of humour and followed me about all the time I cleaned his pen. He always endeavoured to get behind and slightly above me, moving in a series of long effortless hops from perch to perch that were somehow unnerving to see in so large and heavy a bird. Occasionally some sixth sense would warn me that he had sidled up into attacking position and I would spin round to find his huge beak almost touching my nose. More often, though, I would be unsuspecting until I received a resounding whack on my head from a sideways sweep of his beak. I wasn't very happy about this game, as apart from the fact that I never seemed to be the winner, I knew that if ever he were to hit me with a forward lunge instead of a sideways blow my head would probably crack like an eggshell.

Henry lived in one of a series of four walk-through pens with access leading one from the other. His best game of all was to wait until I passed through his pen with a pile of fruit dishes in my arms bound for the monkey pen at the end of the line. Fixing a stern eye on the hornbill, and careful not to turn my back on him, I would close the door, bend under the centre perch and open the door to the adjoining pen. Some time during this procedure, Henry would make a quick feint towards my face with his beak, and as I instinctively ducked he needed to make only one well-aimed blow at the dishes carefully balanced in my arms. As dishes and fruit rolled, bounced and crashed in all directions, the noise almost drowned by my furious comments, Henry would retire to the highest perch with one easy bound, putting his head down low on one side and watching me with sly humour through the fringe of his ridiculous eyelashes; one could almost see him giggling at my confusion. I really was rather relieved when eventually Ken transferred Henry to one of his other zoos at Poole. Not, I may point out, in consideration of my sore head, but to give the hornbill more wing-space!

Among the other animals that Ken brought to Shaldon that first season were an adult male pig-tailed monkey and an adult Celebes crested ape. Both were affected with a certain degree of cage-paralysis, the curse of many primates kept in captivity for any length of time. The cause has been blamed on various things, a lack of proteins, vitamins, sunshine or fresh air, or alternatively coping with a damp and cold climate, caging on concrete floors, or possibly a combination of some or all of these things. But if the cause is as yet uncertain, the result is obvious and distressing: progressive stiffening and loss of use of the hind limbs from the waist down. The disease develops slowly over several months or even years, into the serious stage where the legs appear to be locked at the joints so that the monkey has to use a 'rabbit-hopping' motion to get around. From there it gradually deteriorates into an even worse form where the animal can

216

move only by dragging its legs along behind it.

The Celebes ape was in the very early stage of cage-paralysis, just a slight stiffness to his legs. Piggy, however, had it far more severely, his legs already locked and incapable of moving independently of each other. Ringo, a seven-year-old male chimpanzee at Exmouth, was in an even worse state, unable to move except by pulling himself along with his arms. Ringo had been Ken's special pet since babyhood, and it was breaking his heart to see the steady worsening of the paralysis. Already a primate-expert had examined the chimp and advised Ken to have him destroyed to prevent more suffering.

Many cures had been tried in various zoos and research centres, and the most notable results had been achieved with daily injections of vitamins over a long period. But the cure was expensive and it was an impossible task to give regular injections to such powerful and potentially dangerous animals as adult pig-tails and chimpanzees. Few zoos are lucky enough completely to avoid cases of cage-paralysis in primates. The remainder usually keep quiet about any cases that develop and remove the affected animals from public view, in case they should be regarded as a reflection on the zoo's standard of care. Therefore it's difficult to determine exactly how widespread cage-paralysis is, and unfortunately this over-sensitivity of zoos about any cases that develop on their premises definitely hinders attempts elsewhere to find a proper cure.

When Piggy and the Celebes had been in my care at Shaldon for about a month, I began to wonder whether Abidec would have any effect on their stiff limbs. I had used it successfully as a *preventative* measure against a hundred and one ills in newly-imported animals, but naturally this was no indication that it would be any good as a *curative* medicine, especially in something as fundamental as established paralysis. But, I thought, if it proved to do no good with the paralysis, then at least it would do no harm.

With this in mind, I approached Ken for permission to start dosing the two monkeys with Abidec; after all, he would have to foot the bill. His initial reception to my suggestion was incredulous; but I persisted in the face of his disbelief. 'After all,' I reasoned, 'if Abidec in a normal dose *prevents* cage-paralysis—which I think I've proved with my own

217

animals—then surely there's a theoretical chance that massive doses of Abidec would *cure* it?'

'Christine,' he chided gently, 'you don't seriously think that a simple thing like a vitamin additive would really cure bone malformation, and joints and muscles which have gone totally out of use?'

'No,' I admitted. Put like that, I realised how ridiculous my whole idea was. Then I added stubbornly and illogically: 'But it *might*.'

So Ken decided to humour me and we began the experiment with about as much conviction as a mouse trying to climb a mountain. After a few days with just a trace of Abidec on their food to accustom them to the taste, I put each of the monkeys on a normal daily dose for an adult human. To ensure that each received the correct dose—for they were penned together—I halved a hard-boiled egg and dripped the Abidec on to the yoke; I then directly handed them half the egg each. Apart from being an easy and accurate method of dosing the monkeys, I thought that the protein contained in the egg might also help the cage-paralysis.

After a fortnight, as there was no sign of improvement, I doubled the dose I was giving them, and then took it up to two-and-a-half times the normal adult dose. It was at the end of one month from the start of the treatment—the period which proved to be the turning-point with future tests—that Ken and I agreed we had actual visual evidence that the two monkeys were improving. The Celebes ape had now lost all stiffness in the legs and was moving freely. Piggy's progress was less discernible, but we believed he was becoming more active and energetic. Within another fortnight he started moving his hind legs independently of each other, instead of in the former 'rabbit-hopping' movement.

We watched this latest improvement almost with disbelief. It seemed nothing short of a miracle. Very excited with what we had already achieved, I tried to persuade Ken to start the treatment on the chimpanzee at Exmouth. Ken, however, although he was impressed at the pig-tail's progress, felt that Ringo, completely paralysed from the waist down, was too far gone to respond to such treatment; it would be kinder to have the chimp put down to save further suffering. But when it came to telephoning the vet to come and perform the task, Ken decided he just couldn't do it without giving the Abidec course a try, however hopeless it sounded. Without telling me, he began to give Ringo the treble adult daily dose I had suggested.

During the next two months the improvement in Piggy was steady and satisfying. At the end of three months from the start of treatment he was completely cured. We watched in delight as he leapt around his pen in a near-orgy of activity, giving great leaps from wall to wall, a feat which only a few weeks before had been quite beyond his capabilities. Ken chose that happy moment to tell me that for two months he had been dosing Ringo with Abidec and that during the last two or three weeks the chimp had shown definite signs of reactivity in his paralysed legs.

Ringo's cure took a long time and a lot of persistence. But four months from the start of treatment his cure was complete; he had entirely regained the use of his legs, with no sign of stiffness. As I watched him crashing around his pen at high speed, from wall to rope, leaping from the bars to the ground where he stamped all four feet energetically and screamed lustily in imitation of his Beatle namesake, I reflected that this animal was a far cry from my last sight of him a few months before, a pathetic creature that huddled unmoving for hours in one corner of his pen. This was a moment of such intense pleasure for me that it brought a lump into my throat.

Some while later I developed arthritis in my right elbow. By the time the doctor diagnosed it I had little more than about thirty per cent use of the arm. This was an opportunity to use myself as a guinea-pig, for after our success with the primates my mind had soon turned to the possible effect Abidec would have on arthritis in humans. In two months, using just under treble the normal dose, I had full use of my arm again, and I was able to lift heavy weights as in the past; the constant nagging ache in my elbow had also completely disappeared. I also discovered the valuable fact that there should be no sudden break once the stage of massive dosage is reached; twice I accidentally missed taking a day's dose and I suffered a reaction of the most intense weariness.

Although our experiments with Abidec were very

amateurish and ham-fisted, without X-rays, blood-tests or a proper scientific control anywhere along the line, we personally found the results very exciting and offer them for what they are worth.

By the end of 1970 I could afford once more to start importing on a small scale. In the meantime an import ban had descended on a wide range of mammals during the rabies scare. At the time of writing, although domestic dogs and cats have been allowed into the country on a quarantine basis for the past year we in the zoo world are still waiting with mounting frustration for someone to remember that we are still forbidden, after nearly two years, to import such animals as all monkeys, squirrels, coatimundis, and so on, as well, of course, as all wild cats and dogs. As far as mammals are concerned, in fact, we are just left with a few oddments that we can import, such as otters, elephants, capybara and anteaters; ungulates, although not covered by the rabies ban, are covered by another rule that demands a year's urban quarantine. It not only makes life difficult for the zoo-man and importer in this country, but, far more important, it has made nonsense of countless breeding plans and has also caused the prices of stock already in the country to rocket. Squirrel monkeys, for instance, which I was selling for between £7 and £12 each not long before the ban now fetch £35 each.

So, instead, I have had to concentrate on importing birds and reptiles. In one of the first consignments was a batch of eight baby black-headed caiques. I chose one of the hens as a mate for Jaffa, now just over two years old. He seems to appreciate her company, but I was quite wrong in expecting him to be gentle and affectionate towards her. He behaves just like a feathered Andy Capp, arrogant and bullying his wife constantly, obviously a staunch supporter of male supremacy. If she attempts to take first choice of the fruit, he whacks her very smartly with his beak, whereupon she rolls on to her back in an attitude of complete submission and apology while he stands over her beating his wings and screaming abuse. I leave them to their regular squabbles now; they both seem to enjoy them.

Another early arrival was King Kong, a fledgling macaw. He was an absurd sight when I took him out of the crate.

Apart from a few stubbles on his wings he was absolutely naked. He was really far too young to have been sent from Guyana and I was very doubtful for the first week or two about him surviving. It was a particularly chilly day in late September when he arrived and even with an electric bowl-fire within a few inches of his cage his pink flesh had a blue tinge and he shivered constantly. Although I felt sorry for him, I couldn't help laughing every time I looked in his direction, for he looked exactly like a chicken plucked ready for the oven, but with exceptionally large feet and an outsize hooked beak. He seemed blithely unaware of the fact that he was less than decently dressed, and this is partly how he acquired his name; I started to call him King, after the king with no clothes in the fairy story, but on the second day he gave a squawk that sounded like 'King-Kong', and the name has stuck. It seems quite appropriate when he is clambering ponderously over the budgerigars' cages with his big feet and peering interestedly in at the comparatively tiny inhabitants.

But he is a very gentle monster, exceptionally tame and affectionate. He loves to lie on my lap and let me stroke him, closing his eyes and giving small grunts of pleasure. To everyone's amusement, these grunts are occasionally interspersed with spasms of passionate heavy breathing, as though he is quite overcome with emotion. He is also, I'm afraid, rather a neurotic bird. I had him at home in my warm kitchen, and for the first few weeks after the zoo closed at the end of the season he became used to having me around for most of the time. But I had recently started a zoological livestock agency, which sometimes entailed my collecting and delivering stock to zoos. Two days in succession I was away from home for about eight hours at a stretch, and King Kong immediately went sick. He sat hunched on his perch, ignoring me pointedly, his new blue and yellow feathers seeming to droop despondently. He began to vomit at regular intervals, no food staying down more than a few minutes.

I and the bird expert I hastily consulted considered all manner of dread diseases before we came to the inescapable conclusion that it was a simple matter of emotional disturbance caused by my leaving him alone. As soon as I returned to my former schedule King Kong's recovery was immediate.

To the present moment, he continues to demand as his right all my time, patience and affection. Needless to say, he will never leave the family now.

The zoological agency I started was an immediate success. Instead of selling their surplus stock to dealers at low prices, zoos could now sell direct to other zoos through my agency lists of 'Wants' and 'For Sale', with my charging a small commission on sales.

It was as I was driving across Dartmoor on a very foggy day recently with a vulture in the back of the van that it occurred to me to start wondering back over my life to trace how events had step by step brought me into this situation, rather a peculiar one by the average person's standards. I started laughing to myself as I considered my chances of getting another motorist to help me if I broke down; Dartmoor in a fog is an eerie enough wilderness without coming face to face unexpectedly with an Egyptian vulture. Much the same thought had occurred to me a week or two previously when I had driven through miles of flooded roads with a fully-grown puma in an open wire crate just behind my seat. Apollo, as he was called, was a magnificent animal, the biggest and heaviest-boned puma I have ever seen. At two years old, he had never been in a vehicle in his life, and as it was quite a small van—six hundredweight—there was a stray thought in my mind as I set off on the hundred-mile journey that if he became upset and broke loose from his crate I would have trouble on my hands, or, more literally, a puma in my lap. But Apollo was a model of good behaviour; he sat in the corner of the crate just behind my left ear and breathed heavily down my neck, purring loudly and constantly. Each time I spoke to him he replied with a squeaky miaouw, an incongruous sound from so huge an animal. If I put my hand against the wire of his crate he would rub his head against it like a domestic cat. All our apprehensions about taking the puma in the van were unfounded, although at traffic lights one or two motorists nearly forgot to brake in time when they were faced with a puma staring at them out of the van's back window. The only trouble I had on the journey came not from the puma but from a boxful of tiny gerbils that escaped inside the van and started running over

222

my feet, under the pedals, and across Pinto, my poodle, causing her to leap hysterically into my lap. When one of them ran up the inside of my trouser leg, I had no choice but to stop in a lay-by and, lying half in and half out of the van, catch all the little blighters. All the time I hoped fervently that no-one would stop to see if I was in trouble, for with a very large puma sitting in the back, a dozen gerbils on the loose and a poodle on the point of nervous collapse, it would all take too much explaining.

The animals flowed in with further consignments: tree porcupines, agoutis, tamanduas and many species of birds; a baby King Vulture with a large ungainly body and a passionate cupboard-love for anyone who would hand-feed him with vast quantities of chopped meat until the weight of his bulging crop almost unbalanced him; a tiny baby sloth, which had to be bottle-fed and taken to bed at nights with me to keep it warm; and two adult sloths which displayed an unexpected if slow-motion affection for humans. There were two magnificent giant anacondas, each measuring nearly twenty feet in length, and Fred and Charlie, two baby tapirs. Charlie was a very ticklish animal, and at the first touch of a scrubbing brush during their regular baths he would go into a frenzy of kicking and bucking. But Fred adored wash-time. Scrubbing his side had an extraordinary hypnotic effect on him—his eyes grew glazed, his breathing deepened, and his body leaned slowly until soon he crashed to the floor in a semi-trance. He lay there like a dead animal, his legs sticking out stiffly, his eyes closed in an ecstasy of enjoyment, as I continued to scrub his body vigorously.

But, although I was outwardly content, inside me was a growing ache to be back in the tropics. It was impossible to forget the dream of Saki Island Sanctuary; I *had* to do it, for better or worse. Even while I sternly reminded myself that I had no money for such a project, I remembered that cliché about giant oaks growing from tiny acorns. Lack of money was no excuse for burying my dream; I could start it with next to nothing and build it up from there. First, of course, I would have to save the 'next to nothing', but I don't think it will be too long before I return to a jungle island and the modest release of the first fifty animals into the sanctuary;

and the erection of a handful of primitive bamboo huts for visitors, the forerunner of my planned Bamboo Lodge Hotel for the ever-growing number of people who feel an affinity with wild animals.

One thing makes all the work, the slow saving and the stubborn hope worth while; the anticipation of that great moment when I can open all the cage doors and see my animals living free.